MW01624279

Libraries and Books in Medieval England

Libraries and Books in Medieval England

THE ROLE OF LIBRARIES IN A CHANGING BOOK ECONOMY

The Lyell Lectures for 2018–19

RICHARD SHARPE

edited by James Willoughby

BODLEIAN
LIBRARY
PUBLISHING

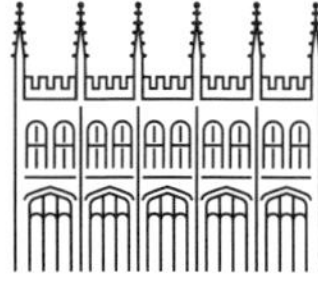

First published in 2023 by the Bodleian Library
Broad Street, Oxford OX1 3BG
www.bodleianshop.co.uk

ISBN 978 1 85124 601 4

Maps by Michael Athanson

Publisher: Samuel Fanous
Managing Editor: Susie Foster
Editor: Janet Phillips
Picture Editor: Leanda Shrimpton
Cover design by Dot Little at the Bodleian Library
Designed and typeset by Lucy Morton of illuminati in 12 on 16 Bembo
Printed and bound by Gomer Press Limited on 120 gsm Edixion Offset paper

British Library Catalogue in Publishing Data
A CIP record of this publication is available from the British Library

Contents

Foreword

I came to work in the Bodleian as Keeper of Special Collections and Western Manuscripts in 2003. One of the many things which attracted me to the post was the thought of working with the great scholars at Oxford who toiled in the field of the study of manuscripts and early books. High on the list of people I was keen to meet was Richard Sharpe.

It was not long after I actually arrived in Bodley that I met Richard, and he soon became a familiar figure that I would spot in the reading rooms of the Old Library and in the New Bodleian (he can be described accurately as a 'super-user' of the Bodleian), but I seemed to meet him most often just in the street as he was coming to or from his office in the History Faculty, then to be found in the old Indian Institute building on the corner of Catte Street and Holywell Street. It was a hot summer that year, so it wasn't odd to see him wearing shorts and a striped shirt with only a couple of buttons done up, but later that year I realized that this was what he wore no matter what time of year or climactic conditions. A few months later I received an invitation to be his guest at the Dorothy Dinner, Wadham's great feast to commemorate its founding benefactor, which was my first experience of an Oxford occasion of this kind. It was a very memorable and highly enjoyable evening, and at some point in the course of the dinner

Richard suggested a project to create a digital third edition of Neil Ker's *Medieval Libraries of Great Britain*, a notion that was close to my heart as I was a former student of Andrew G. Watson, Ker's literary executor, who was responsible for the supplement to the second edition of *MLGB*, and who had of course retired to Oxford (another draw for me to move from Edinburgh).

Over the succeeding years there would be many lunches and even more stand-up meetings in Broad Street and Catte Street with Richard over this and many other related projects (especially those concerning the medieval charters, Oxford printing in the seventeenth century, Irish manuscripts, among numerous others). One such discussion brought us to apply together to the Andrew W. Mellon Foundation for a grant to digitize the printed editions of *Medieval Libraries of Great Britain*, and the associated index cards that Neil Ker had used to compile the first edition, and to link the resulting data set with records from the Corpus of Medieval Library Catalogues. The application for funding was successful, and the resultant digital resource, still hosted by the Bodleian and known as *MLGB* 3, has been truly transformational in broadening scholarship in this field. One sees the searches that *MLGB* 3 made possible throughout these Lyell Lectures. When I became Bodley's Librarian in 2014, I also became chair of the Lyell Electors, and it was an obvious thing for the Electors to ask Richard (then one of our number) to step outside the room, so that we could formally invite him to deliver the Lectures, which he eventually did in the spring of 2019.

Somehow Richard managed to balance all of these multiple projects simultaneously, to continue his teaching, especially teaching with manuscripts and medieval documents, and to continue his prodigious research agenda, and to see so much of this research appear in scholarly publications. One routinely encounters in Oxford individuals who are formidable scholars, but rarely in someone who was also an industrious project director, fund-raiser, teacher and doctoral supervisor. Listening to these Lectures, and reading them now, one must remember that Richard Sharpe was also progressing an impressive array of other projects at the same time, each to a similar intensity of scholarship and erudition. To say that news of his death came as a shock and a blow is a supreme understatement, and I cannot quite believe that I won't bump into him outside the Clarendon Building again.

The Lyell Electors and the Bodleian Libraries are extremely grateful to Dr James Willoughby for seeing the text of Richard's Lectures through the press, and we are pleased to be able to publish them, and to continue the Bodleian's long association with this great scholar.

Richard Ovenden
Bodley's Librarian

Preface

BOOKS, LIKE THEIR OWNERS, are vulnerable at all times to extinction. Libraries have always been raised against dangers from fire, flood or pillage, or the slower road of attrition through loss, loan or simple wear and tear. In England the defining moment of jeopardy was the dissolution of the religious houses under King Henry VIII, an act that swept away the institutional setting for hundreds of thousands of books and made their survival a matter of chance. But it is a cultural reflex of our own that summons a monk with a quill and a cloistered library of ancient books as the sole agents for the descent of literature in the medieval West. It is as if the cataclysm of the dissolution and the loss of the monastic heritage has only sharpened the sense in England that a medieval library was a monastic library. The intention for this volume is to offer a corrective. It proposes that the medieval book economy in England was more vigorous and ran more widely than the traditional view would make it appear; and, albeit the evidence is fragmentary for almost every question that might be posed, the difficulty of reaching conclusions on the origins of the book trade or the number of books in private ownership should not starve the attempt.

The matter of this volume was first delivered at the Bodleian Library as the University of Oxford's Lyell Lectures for 2018–19. Richard

Sharpe's sudden death on 21 March 2020, at the age of sixty-six, may have robbed this volume of its chance to be seen into the press by its author, but it stands none the less as an eloquent witness to a master's view of the territory. Richard Sharpe's name is the latest in the roll of honour of those who have sought to understand and give shape to the matter of the descent of manuscripts in England. How far this knowledge can be related meaningfully to the pursuit of learning in the Middle Ages is an important and difficult question that it will remain to others to investigate. Here, though, is a book of maps to inform that journey, left by a tireless explorer.

As these pages make clear, it was precisely because the process of secularization came earlier to England and the dispersals of books were more thorough than almost anywhere else in Europe that provenance research in Great Britain has had a head start. It has been proceeding now in what might be called a scientific manner for more than a century. That any sort of theoretical statement may be made on the circulation of knowledge in the Middle Ages is owing entirely to two projects of long gestation, conceived of together and only now reaching their fulfilment.

'Dr M.R. James has been before us almost everywhere and his discoveries are on nearly every page of this book', wrote Neil Ker in his foreword to *Medieval Libraries of Great Britain*, one great name commemorating another. It was James (1862–1936), provost of King's College in Cambridge and later provost of Eton, who first began to take systematic notice of surviving books that bore clues to their medieval provenance, and who also first saw the value that medieval catalogues have for the study of the descent of manuscripts. The two streams of evidence increasingly came to connect in his own work as he began to appreciate their importance not only for the sort of antiquarian research that he enjoyed, but more generally for what they could say to the transmission of culture and the history of thought.

It was pioneering work, and perhaps there was more than a simple veil of modesty in James's comment in *Ancient Libraries of Canterbury and Dover* (1903) that 'I do not know how far these remarks will go towards convincing anyone that researches of this kind are worth the time spent on them; if they fail entirely to do so, I shall have to do as best I can without the sympathy of my critics.'

If the name of M.R. James attaches lustre to Cambridge, the story is otherwise an Oxonian one. The men who came after James, beginning together in the 1930s, formed a golden generation in Oxford. The four protagonists were Sir Roger Mynors (1903–1989), then a classics don at Balliol College, who had first known M.R. James at Eton and remained on friendly terms, Richard Hunt (1908–1979), subsequently Keeper of Western Manuscripts in the Bodleian, Christopher Cheney (1906–1987), then Reader in Diplomatic in Oxford, and Neil Ker (1908–1982), university Reader in Palaeography. The then recent publication by Maurice Powicke, Regius Professor of Modern History, of *The Medieval Books of Merton College* (1931), a substantial offshoot of his work on scholastic history, must have been a considerable inspiration. The notion of an index of manuscripts by medieval provenance came from Cheney, who wrote to Hunt about it in November 1937. It chimed with Hunt and Mynors' work on *Registrum Anglie*, a union catalogue compiled towards the end of the thirteenth century by the Grey Friars of Oxford. Cheney fostered and encouraged the work, Hunt and Mynors contributed their knoweldge, but it was Ker who took the chief part in the enterprise and it was under his name that the first edition of *Medieval Libraries of Great Britain* appeared in 1941. The Corpus of British Medieval Library Catalogues was a sister enterprise, discussed in the 1930s and never forgotten, but for which Mynors, Ker and Hunt only gathered a formal committee in 1976; the project was adopted by the British Academy in 1979.

The inheritor of this tradition was Richard Sharpe. Mynors was the figure Sharpe most closely resembled in his own composition as a scholar. Like Mynors, he was by formation a classicist, and his interest in old books began in what they could offer to the matter of textual transmission. Like Mynors, he was a textual critic and editor, at home in the Latin of the late antique to late medieval periods. Unlike Mynors, he had interests, fostered by his university post as Reader in Diplomatic, in non-literary texts and documents. He possessed a historian's sensibility and a deep historical memory, able to throw thrillingly unexpected light on large questions from the closest of close readings. His range in print extended from discussion of the composition of the Council of Serdica of 343 CE to the nineteenth-century book trade, via the early Irish Church, Anglo-Norman royal diplomatic, medieval bibliography, and early-modern learned correspondence. He was an extraordinarily prolific scholar, another way in which he diverged from the example of Mynors; in the large extent of his publication record he much more resembled Neil Ker. And, although he never thought of himself as a palaeographer, he was, like Ker, a miniaturist who could step back and see an entire landscape.

Professor Sharpe paid tribute to Neil Ker in his first lecture, noting that James Lyell himself had nominated Ker to be the first Lyell Reader in Bibliography, in 1952–3. Sharpe confessed that, while he had never known Ker, who died in August 1982 following a fall while picking bilberries on the slopes of Schiehallion, he did remember how the news was posted along with a photograph at the Duke Humfrey Reserve in the Bodleian, the library where Ker had been for fifty years a key member of the manuscript-reading community. The medievalist Margaret Gibson (1938–1994) – like Ker, from Edinburgh – was standing beside the photo and talking to readers about him. It was she who, six years later, as secretary of the British Academy committee that was overseeing the Corpus of British Medieval Library Catalogues, 'first inveigled' Sharpe into working on some of the Benedictine libraries. His subsequent appointment in 1990 to the Readership in Diplomatic in the University of Oxford recognized a gifted philologist with the forensic capacities required for serious study of medieval charters and documents. Short weeks after that appointment he was invited by Joseph Trapp (1925–2005), director of the Warburg Institute and chair of the project committee, to become the first general editor of the Corpus.

While he may not have known Ker, Richard Sharpe was on terms of friendship with Sir Roger Mynors, and recalled his debts to him at the start of his second lecture. He came to know Mynors in the mid-1980s, when working as an assistant editor for the *Dictionary of British Latin from Medieval Sources*. Mynors would join the lexicographers for tea in the Bodleian staff canteen, and Sharpe recalled how they discussed together Sharpe's aspiration to produce what was eventually published as his *Handlist of Latin Writers of Great Britain and Ireland before 1540* (1997). Some months after Mynors' death in October 1989, Sharpe received a suitcase of material designated to come to him. The papers inside included the typescript of Mynors' edition of the *Registrum Anglie* and other related studies, and a small attaché case containing hundreds of little cards recording manuscript shelfmarks for works of British writers, something that would inform the work for the *Handlist of Latin Writers*. He also inherited a paper printout from microfilm which comprised an unassigned medieval catalogue of books under headings for eighteen authors, each with a list of titles, each title accompanied by one or more shelfmarks. This unnamed catalogue had long retained its enigma. Turning to Ker's *Medieval Libraries of Great Britain*, Sharpe found shelfmarks which matched the entries in two series, Arabic and Roman, and was able to identify the catalogue as belonging to St Mary's abbey in York. The discovery allowed him to bring the catalogue into his own volume of the Corpus, on the shorter

Benedictine catalogues, then in an advanced state of preparation – and, coming in as York, it did not disturb the numbering of documents. Sharpe, a son of the city, in recounting this story at the start of his second lecture, said that he felt his angel had been busy.

It marked an early success in his involvement with a series that came strongly to bear his impress. When he began, the first volume of the series was already in print – disagreements between the author and the project committee over its shape had demonstrated the need for a general editor. He made reforms and oversaw the next fifteen volumes with acuity, great energy, and a dauntless precision in his critical reading. Not the least of his reforms was to establish a cumulative listing of the authors and works identified in separate volumes of the series, which he dubbed the List of Identifications. It was designed to serve as a ready reckoner for editors and to ensure consistency in citation across volumes. The prospect of creating ghosts or duplicating entries for the same work – the need to keep hold of the evidence, always a defining concern of his scholarship – gave him a strong sense of responsibility in ensuring the accurate identification of texts. Equally, Sharpe's long experience of curating the List gave him an instinctive sense of when an editor's identification might be at fault. For, while I have suggested that he was the latest great figure in an Oxford tradition that goes back to Mynors, Ker and Hunt, he stood also in a longer bibliographical lineage. His *Handlist of Latin Writers* sites him at the latest end of a tradition that goes back to Thomas Tanner (1674–1735), John Pits (1560–1616), and ultimately to the Tudor bibliographers active at the time of the dissolutions, John Leland (1506–1552) and John Bale (1495–1563).

The List will be published in the final volume of indexes to the Corpus, but is also available through *MLGB*3, the digital third edition of *Medieval Libraries of Great Britain*, which was envisaged and brought about by Richard Sharpe. Hosted by the Bodleian, this resource, which has been freely available since 2015, is described and discussed in the following pages so there is no need to expand on the subject here. Suffice it to say that *MLGB3* unites the evidence of provenanced books and medieval catalogues in a way that allows the evidence to be approached in an integrative manner. It is possible to search by author or title across the whole data set, opening to scholars the means of discovering quickly all known copies of a particular author or work, extant or attested, that can be provenanced to a particular medieval library. It may be said to have finally fulfilled the ambition of the sister projects' originators in a way that none of them could have foreseen.

It is a sadness that Professor Sharpe himself did not live to see the completion of the Corpus. But he knew from typescript the three volumes yet to be printed and used their data in these lectures. His Lyell Lectures therefore represent the first attempt, after a century of enterprise in providing the materials, to form a general statement from the totality of the surviving evidence.

Watching Richard Sharpe at work was like watching a trapeze artist or acrobat: one could only stand back in admiration, and wonder what combination of dedication and natural abilities could have produced such an effect. A scholar of such extraordinary capacities could never have had the time he needed for everything he wanted to do. Alongside the Corpus, his editions of the royal *acta* of Kings William II and Henry I will stand as lasting monuments of his energy and vision, and it is greatly to be hoped that they can be brought to completion. We shall not now have his edition of Goscelin of Saint-Bertin, an author he had long admired, or his investigation into the *opera* of Caesarius of Arles (which he suspected had been over-counted). A gigantic task for the future was to have been no less than an investigation of the authority of all the Latin Fathers: he had planned to apply to patristic literature the evidence-based approach he pioneered for medieval texts. In all of his scholarship, his first concern was to find the bedrock, which he did by questioning the evidence and the basis of evidence. He knew that transmission is a concessionary process, and he kept in mind every context for that process, fixing acute attention on manuscripts and the ways they have been read, propagated and husbanded. Books represent texts, and texts die without them. There have been few British scholars who have united such a penetrating perception of books and texts together as Richard Sharpe. It is a consolation that in these Lyell Lectures he was able to turn his mature attention to the matter of the medieval libraries of England.

Professor Sharpe was planning no great revision of his text. I have compared his typescript to recordings of his lectures, and where they differed have adjudicated in what I hope is the right direction. Smoothing the text for the press has otherwise involved only light touches. I have also taken the liberty of supplying the notes and indexes. In preparing this volume I have benefited much by the expertise and good advice of Professor Ralph Hanna. I know that Professor Sharpe would have wanted to thank his friends Cristina Dondi and Bill Stoneman for support and discussion at the time when he was writing these lectures. Thanks are also due to Michael Athanson, of the Bodleian, for producing the maps used in Figures 1 & 2. I am grateful to Professor Sharpe's heirs for permission to proceed with this publication and for the kind assistance of Bodleian Library Publishing.

Professor Sharpe prefaced his first two Lyell Lectures with warm recollections of Roger Mynors, Margaret Gibson and Joseph Trapp. He left a note that he intended to dedicate this volume to their memory.

James Willoughby
Oxford

List of Illustrations

Abbreviations

Reference is made throughout to catalogues and other booklists published in the Corpus of British Medieval Library Catalogues (CBMLC) by the alphanumerical system which is conventional in that series. Such references are designated by one or two letters to indicate the volume (the volumes arranged by species of institution), followed by a number to indicate a particular document in that volume, and then another number to specify an entry within that document, following the form 'B1. 123'. The letter-marks are as follows.

A *The Libraries of the Augustinian Canons*, ed. T. Webber and A.G. Watson, CBMLC, 6 (London, 1998).

B *English Benedictine Libraries: The Shorter Catalogues*, ed. R. Sharpe, J.P. Carley, R.M. Thomson and A.G. Watson, CBMLC, 4 (London, 1996).

BA *St Augustine's Abbey, Canterbury*, ed. B.C. Barker-Benfield, CBMLC, 13, 3 vols (London, 2008).

BC The Libraries of the Cathedral Priory of Christ Church, Canterbury (forthcoming).

BD The Libraries of Durham Cathedral Priory (forthcoming).

BM *Dover Priory*, ed. W.P. Stoneman, CBMLC, 5 (London, 1999).

BP *Peterborough Abbey*, ed. K. Friis-Jensen and J.M.W. Willoughby, CBMLC, 8 (London, 2001).

C *The Libraries of the Carthusians*, ed. A.I. Doyle, CBMLC, 9 (London, 2001).

F The Friars' Libraries, ed. K.W. Humphreys, CBMLC, 1 (London, 1990); a second edition is forthcoming.

G *The Libraries of the Cistercians, Gilbertines and Premonstratensians*, ed. D.N. Bell, CBMLC, 3 (London, 1992).

H *The Libraries of King Henry VIII*, ed. J.P. Carley, CBMLC, 7 (London, 2000).

K *Henry of Kirkestede, Catalogus de libris autenticis et apocrifis*, ed. R.H. Rouse and M.A. Rouse, CBMLC, 11 (London, 2004).

P *The Libraries of the Cistercians, Gilbertines and Premonstratensians*, ed. D.N. Bell, CBMLC, 3 (London, 1992).

R *Registrum Anglie de libris doctorum et auctorum veterum*, ed. R.H. Rouse and M.A. Rouse, CBMLC, 2 (London, 1991).

S *Scottish Libraries*, ed. J. Higgitt, with an introduction by J. Durkan, CBMLC, 12 (London, 2006).

SC *The Libraries of the Secular Cathedrals*, ed. J.M.W. Willoughby and N.L. Ramsay, CBMLC, 17 (London, 2023) [SC1–]; and *The Libraries of Collegiate Churches*, ed. J.M.W. Willoughby, CBMLC, 15, 2 vols (London, 2013) [SC201–].

SH *Hospitals, Towns, and the Professions*, ed. N.L. Ramsay and J.M.W. Willoughby, CBMLC, 14 (London, 2009).

SS *Syon Abbey*, ed. V.A. Gillespie, CBMLC, 9 (London, 2001).

UC *The University and College Libraries of Cambridge*, ed. P.D. Clarke, with an introduction by R. Lovatt, CBMLC, 10 (London, 2002).

UO *The University and College Libraries of Oxford*, ed. R.M. Thomson, with the assistance of J.G. Clark, CBMLC, 16, 2 vols (London, 2015).

Z *The Libraries of the Cistercians, Gilbertines and Premonstratensians*, ed. D.N. Bell, CBMLC, 3 (London, 1992).

ONE

Medieval Libraries of Great Britain

TO HELP UNDERSTAND the transmission of culture in the Middle Ages we have medieval books to examine and we conceptualize the libraries which held them; but the question What is a library? is always begged. For eighty years there has been a ready-made answer in the form of a handbook by Neil Ker, *Medieval Libraries of Great Britain*, known commonly by the abbreviation *MLGB*.[1] This work announces itself as a list of surviving books that carry evidence of their medieval ownership, organized by provenance, where that is an institution. The word *library* is equated with institutional ownership.

Books themselves can tell us much about their former institutional homes but one needs to learn to listen carefully: interpretation has come to rely on a set of assumptions about the status of medieval libraries which might not be helpful. Library catalogues drawn up in the Middle Ages can tell more, since they are documents that really speak to the question of what works a library held and how the books were organized. These two bodies of evidence are complementary: the documentary sources do much more to depict a library as a whole, but comparison with the surviving books allows us to add material detail to some of the books described in the documents, enriching the written record. The documents give us the setting to enlarge our view from individual books to whole collections.

My concern in this volume is to consider how we might get from the evidence of provenanceable books and medieval booklists to a lively understanding of the diversity of medieval libraries in England over time (I do not seek to create a narrative from the exiguous surviving evidence from Wales or from Scotland). For this reason I begin with the sources of evidence, the books and the booklists. Two questions are raised on the back of this discussion: simply put, where do library books come from and where do they go to? One cannot simply by looking differentiate a library book from other books for study. Even if it happens to contain library markings, the same book might have been a personal book and then an institutional book and then a personal book again. These movements are very important for how we reconstruct what I call the book economy in which libraries were but a part – how large or how small a part is something which I think has not been articulated very well. The mere existence of *MLGB* may have fostered a tendency to exaggerate libraries' share in the overall book economy. That will be the focus of the middle third of this volume.

Building on the evidence discussed in the first two chapters and the questions aired in the middle two, the final third of this volume will outline the history of libraries in England as they evolved over a period of some five hundred years, from pre-Conquest book collections (such as we can know them at all) to early Tudor libraries (inasmuch as we can say such a thing existed distinct from late medieval libraries). The period is a long one, and the tools we use, especially *MLGB*, have a tendency to flatten the evidence into lists that do not reflect the real dimension of time in the coming and going of individual books, which were not always new when acquired by an institution and did not necessarily remain in the same institution from the time of their production to the institutions' extinction (in most cases) in England in the 1530s and 1540s.

To encapsulate the argument at the outset, I offer three points for consideration. First, libraries in medieval England (and everywhere else) took many forms, and we must never talk about *the* medieval library as if medieval libraries conformed to one definable type. Second, the libraries of medieval England were not static, still less cumulative, but often changing, despite the incontrovertible fact that some books managed to stay in place for more than five centuries. The books we have do not always speak for those we have not. Third, we cannot think about libraries without thinking about the books themselves. While there were episodes when we can perceive this or that library as a planned collection, with managed production, which in England was chiefly a phenomenon of the early twelfth century, most libraries at most times represented the unplanned migration of books between personal ownership and institutional ownership, a migration that often proved temporary, chaining of books notwithstanding. There are two considerations to be held alongside these three points: we do not really understand how the demand for books was met in the Middle Ages outside the specific context of curricular books in a university setting; and we certainly do not understand the attrition of the book supply in diverse contexts over the long period under review.

Neil Ker's *Medieval Libraries of Great Britain*, a Royal Historical Society handbook, has been a classic of historical bibliography since it was first published in 1941. The story of how the work was created is well known through the biographical memoirs of four protagonists, Roger Mynors (1903–1989), then a classics don at Balliol College, who had the idea; Richard Hunt (1908–1979), his former student and subsequently Keeper of Western Manuscripts in the Bodleian, who encouraged it; Christopher Cheney (1906–1987), then Reader in Diplomatic in Oxford, who got cards printed to manage the work and found a publisher for it in wartime; and Neil Ker himself (1908–1982), of Magdalen College, University Reader in Palaeography, who alone remained in Oxford during the war years as a hospital orderly.[2] The idea rose out of Mynors' work on *Registrum Anglie*, a union catalogue listing copies of select authors mainly from monastic libraries, compiled by the Oxford Franciscans in the late thirteenth century.[3] Mynors in the 1930s wanted to be able to test whether particular libraries could be shown to have held copies of the works catalogued as theirs in the *Registrum*, so the notion of an index of manuscripts by provenance emerged, albeit with only the briefest indication of the works in each book. Writing to Richard Hunt in 1937, Mynors referred to it as an index of monastic libraries, and monastic libraries have continued to be seen as the dominant thread.

It was a major achievement, involving the reading of a great many pages of descriptive catalogues and the filling out of cards for each book with evidence of its medieval provenance. Never before had provenance research pulled together so much information that had been so long dispersed. The early dissolution of the monasteries in England had a devastating effect, both in destruction and in scatter, something which much of Europe avoided where secularization came much later and in a different form.[4] Because of the early dispersion and destruction, this kind of provenance research began sooner in England than in Italy, France or Germany. Early work on English provenances, such as that by M.R. James on Bury St Edmunds or Henri Omont on Llanthony, focused on libraries that had left large caches of survivors, comparable to the preservation of large religious libraries from France and Germany, or they depended on cross-matching survivors with entries in the large medieval library catalogues that had already attracted attention, such as the early-fourteenth-century catalogue of Canterbury cathedral priory.[5] Now, by dividing up the reading of descriptive catalogues between five pairs of hands – the fifth man being Richard Hunt's friend Jock Liddell, of Corpus Christi College, who would soon leave Oxford for Athens and a more colourful career as a novelist – the whole range of data from England, Scotland and Wales was brought together, wherever a book had been described that could be provenanced on what Ker would call positive evidence.

The core information was collected on index cards during the years 1938 to 1940. During late 1940 and 1941 Ker in Oxford took on the job of writing out the necessary information for the printer and so in effect of designing the printed page, which has worked extraordinarily well ever since. The first edition was published in 1941, a second and much augmented edition in 1964, and a supplement in 1987. In 2009 (the year before the next date in the progression) work began on a third edition of *MLGB* to digitize the 1964 edition and the supplement, *MLGB*2 and *MLGB*2+ as we know them, with a view to a third edition and an electronic version that could do much more, *MLGB*3, hosted by the Bodleian Library.[6]

The information on each individual book is presented with much concision in one line, a brilliant compression of information that works for the eye and has been found user-friendly to a remarkable degree. It has been imitated in similar projects in Belgium, Germany and (though far from complete) France. A typical entry will appear as follows:

> NORWICH, Norfolk. *Benedictine cathedral priory of Holy Trinity*
> Oxford, Balliol College, *e*300B. J. Sarisburiensis, s. xiv–xiv/xv X.clxxxxiii

Here, a surviving manuscript from Norwich cathedral priory is represented by its modern holding institution and shelfmark, prefaced with an italic letter code to show the nature of the evidence for provenance (here, *e*, standing for *ex libris*), then an indication of contents, date, and finally the Norwich cathedral mark, being here book no. 193 in the X class, which contained volumes received from Cardinal Adam Easton (as will be discussed below). The difficulties involved in coaxing such a layout through the press must have been very great. For

FIGURE 1 Map showing the distribution of identified books with provenance according to their medieval homes (*large dots*), as against medieval institutions from which no books are known (*small dots*)

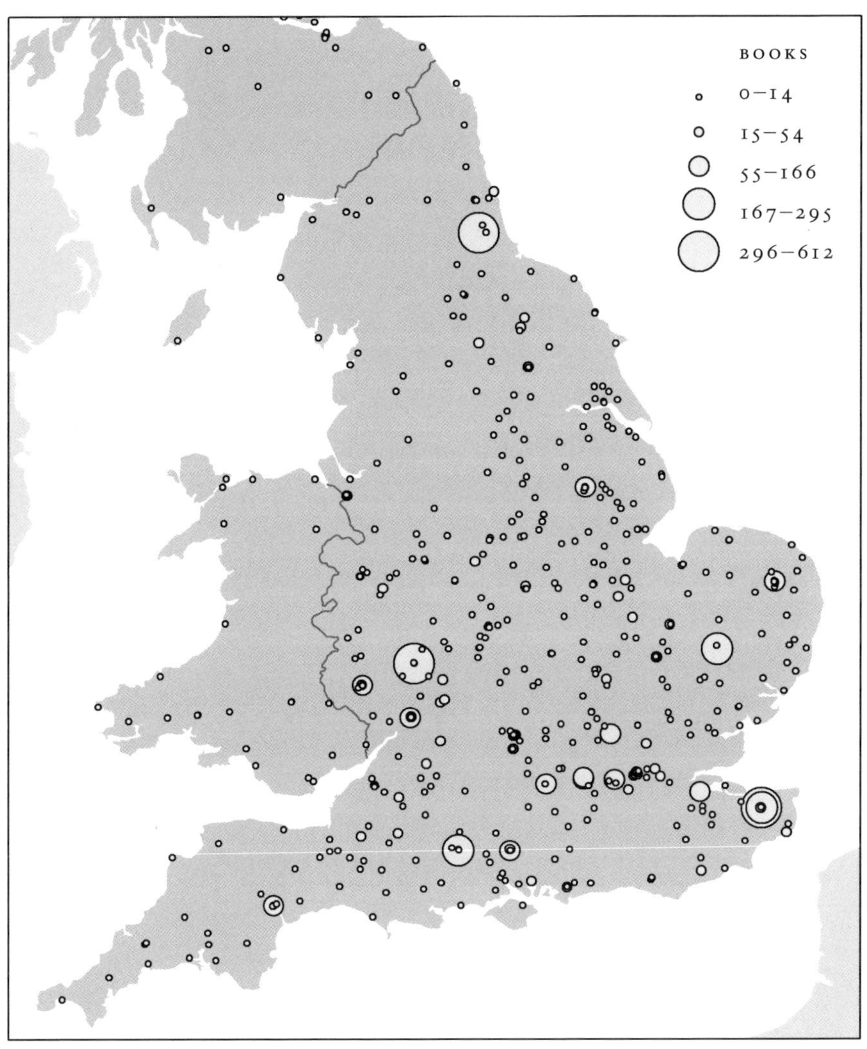

FIGURE 2 Map representing relative extents of survival of identified books with provenance

the online *MLGB3*, digital presentation offers scope for more. While there is clear benefit in retaining the familiar and helpfully concise presentation, the new medium can more easily allow the user to open up the primary single-line entry and see more detail behind it. There is educative potential in being able to see, for example, the wording of an inscription of ownership, perhaps having an image alongside; or to have further detail on contents or on post-dissolution ownership; or to have an explanation of certain ambiguities that might exist around a particular provenance rather than accept the curt question mark signalled in the printed edition.

Digital presentation also allows data to be harvested more easily. *MLGB* brings together extant books with evidence of provenance from far and wide. It is possible to plot these identified books on a map, as for FIGURE 1. The map shows a large dot for every institution from which a book has been recorded in *MLGB3*; the small dots represent institutions with the potential to appear but from which no books have been recorded. It is possible to map religious houses, regardless of whether they appear in *MLGB* or not, but no attempt has been made to map guilds or parish churches or other sorts of institution that might have held small collections of books in the later Middle Ages and from which a book or two might have survived with evidence of provenance. The map is a reminder that our information is woefully incomplete even at a basic level. A rather difficult question to answer follows from this, namely: what is the most conspicuous gap? Is there some large and prosperous religious house from which no books have been identified? The map shows that there are areas with no relevant institutions as well as areas with institutions but without provenanceable survivors. There are areas, in the north of England for example, in central Wales, or the moors in the south-west, where there were no institutions. But there are also areas where there were many institutions but no surviving books. That is the case, for example, immediately west of Oxford, where one might have expected loose books to have been gathered up; but they were not. One might arrange the data differently, omitting the places with no books and using differentially sized dots to show institutions from which more or fewer books have been identified (FIGURE 2). (The dots here do not increase in scale proportionately or the biggest would have become very big indeed.)

It ought to be admitted that the definition applied to a library in *MLGB* has its problems. Ker included service books, whose relationship to a library is debatable, but he excluded cartularies and registers, which held no interest for him.[7] Most of the time, and there can be no complaint, *MLGB* is used simply as a ready reckoner to check whether this or that book, of interest to the inquirer at the time, has an established provenance and on what grounds. In the other direction, one may browse it to find libraries represented by a substantial number of identified survivors, where there is a body of material evidence that invites further work. Ker himself wrote a fine article focused in this way on interpreting the evidence of books from Norwich cathedral priory, with 126 surviving books entered in *MLGB3*.[8]

The marks in a good many Norwich books have a commonplace appearance, E. xxiii, N. lxi, X.cliii, which are open to several possible interpretations, something that shows how a shelfmark can reveal not only the fact that there was organization in a particular library – not all libraries show this – but that, with enough examples, it is possible to work out the pattern and predict how many books there were at the height of that system (FIGURE 3).[9] In the case of Norwich, Ker showed that the letter-marks increase progressively over time, that books marked A were those that had survived the great fire in 1272, when the citizens of Norwich burnt and looted the priory. Books in the priory church survived and were marked A, and new books acquired after 1272 were marked with letters B to L; the precise significance of these classes is not apparent, but as they grew larger, further letters beyond L

Incipit tractatus utilis super totum officium misse editus et compilatus per fratrem Bernardum de Parentinis ordinis predicatorum provincie Tholosane et conventus Orthesii de Vasconia sicut legit in Albia pluribus auditoribus solempnibus doctoribus religiosis bacallariis et clericis Anno domini millesimo ccc xxxix°. Et incepit feria tercia post omnes sanctos accepto thema quod sequitur de evangelio illius diei et terminavit usque ad finem sancti Petri martiris in [illegible] et fo. ii seq. Prologus.

Romanam clamitat sapiens quod perscrutator maiestatis opprimetur a gloria. Propterea nemo existimet hoc officium sufficienter expositum, ne forte cum opus humanum extulerit divinum extenuet sacramentum. Sunt enim in hoc officio tot tanta tam preclara mistica involuta ut nullus eorum sensum penetrat aut sufficiat explicare nisi unctione spiritus sancti fuerit plenius [illegible]. Quapropter ego reus et nescius non prevalens lippientibus oculis solem in rota conspicere tanti et tam preclari misterii maiestatem quam per speculum et in enigmate in visu suo intuens, preter penetrans ad interiora sed pre foribus sedens in vestibulo post messores boni spicas colligens non sufficienter ut volui, sed feci quod potui diligenter, presertim cum tunc actu in officio lectorie quod vires meas excedebat fuerim occupatus. Et quidem minor in singulis dimissis ad singula vix potui meditanda concipere nec concepta dictare aut scribere stilo rudi. Quo circa non solum imploro lectorem benivolum sed etiam liberum desidero correctorem, me et omnia correctioni sancte matris Romane ecclesie subiciens, necnon et ordinis mei sancti qui semper veritatem docuit et dilexit. Hanc intendo solum huius opusculi apud homines expectans ut ad piissimum iudicem pro me peccatore devotas fundant preces qui liquido novit qua cordis intencione tractatum hunc egerim et si non multis saltem aliquibus aut michi soli vel in modico profuturum. In quo per ordinem omnia prosequor movendo dubia aliqua utilia accidentaliter interposita in quibus ut in pluribus sequor sentenciam doctoris preclarissimi sancti Thome nostri ordinis cuius doctrina lucida ut sole luna tota ecclesia illustratur. In quibusdam autem aliis et in casibus iuris sequor viam [illegible] et doctorum meliorum nichil addens de capite singulare. Et ut apercius totius huius tractatus processus legentibus appareat pro modo prologi hic premitto quod hoc opus in tres partes dividitur principales. In quarum prima agitur de quibusdam precedentibus que hoc sacramentum reddunt venerabile que sunt quinque ut inferius apparebit. In secunda agitur de hoc sacramentum perficientibus quod ipsum reddunt [illegible] [illegible]. In tercia et ultima agitur de diversis periculis circa hoc sacramentum were added over time, and letter-class X, represented by six surviving books, goes up to X.ccxxviii. Those up to X.clxxxxiii (and potentially beyond) had belonged to Cardinal Adam Easton, who died in Rome in 1396, and were shipped from Italy to England in 1407, eleven years after his death, when a single hand entered the Norwich marks in them. This number of X.clxxxxiii is in Oxford, Balliol College, MS. 300B, a fourteenth-century copy of John of Salisbury's *Policraticus*; defects in its text were made good in a late-fourteenth-century hand. Roger Mynors, who drew up the Balliol catalogue, showed the letter-mark and partially erased inscription to Ker, who at once identified the book as from Cardinal Easton's library; Ker drew it to the attention of Billy Pantin, of Oriel College, who responded with a photograph of a letter in Easton's name, in the archive at Westminster Abbey, in the same hand as the corrector: perhaps more likely Easton himself than a clerk working for him in two very different capacities? 'Happy the maker of catalogues who has such friends!', wrote Mynors.[10] (There is one higher number, X.ccxxviii, on a Norwich book, CUL MS. Ii. 3. 32, which might allow us to infer that Easton's library, shipped in seven hogsheads, comprised at least that number of volumes when it was absorbed by the abbey.) After the book reached Norwich and was assigned a letter-mark, the title of the work was written at the front, soon followed by reference to *Henricus* and a price in marks, now illegible. Then, in Mynors' words 'not much later', a new *ex libris*, 'Liber domus de Balliolo Oxonie', was added. The example may therefore serve for specimens of personal books that become institutional books – or in this case a substantial personal library, which would have its own story if we had enough evidence to read it – which is explored

FIGURE 3 An *ex libris* from Norwich cathedral priory with a note of donation from Br. John Elyngham and the class-mark 'M. lxxvj', in the same hand as other books with M marks (Oxford, Bodleian Library, MS. Bodl. 787, fol. 1r)

further in Chapter 3 below. The book migrated from Norwich to Oxford, a point which anticipates the discussion of Chapter 4, that books with sound provenance-evidence from a certain date may none the less move elsewhere.

This example also illustrates one of the larger limitations of *MLGB*. For the first edition in 1941 Ker omitted major collections still *in situ*. For the second edition in 1964 he changed policy as regards cathedrals, so that the cathedral collections of Durham, Hereford, Salisbury and Worcester found a place in *MLGB*2 but not the medieval colleges of Oxford and Cambridge. So, for Balliol, 19 manuscripts from the medieval college appeared in the original edition, 22 in the second edition, all books that had long since left the college. For the manuscripts still at Balliol, the first edition simply refers to Coxe's catalogue of Oxford college libraries (1852) and the second adds reference to Mynors' catalogue (1963). In his introduction Ker names ten colleges that 'have still an appreciable number of their medieval books'.[11] The policy understood that every scholar interested in such things would know which colleges still had their medieval manuscripts. This may still be true within Oxford, but it is unhelpful to the world beyond. It also conceals the difficulty of knowing which of the medieval manuscripts now in a college library had been there since the Middle Ages. Balliol has perhaps 350 medieval manuscripts today (the use of duplicating marks such as 300A and 300B makes the numbering less transparent than it might be). The intention has always been that *MLGB*3 should add the books for university colleges which have been *in situ* since the Middle Ages. For Balliol alone some 290 manuscripts have been added to the tally. As we shall see, this change across the colleges as a whole will make a substantial difference to the perception of the data.

Another limitation is the treatment of printed books. Given that evidence for manuscripts is taken down to the dissolution of the monasteries in 1540, *MLGB* could include books printed at any time in a period of more than eighty years since Gutenberg began the printing revolution. Ker recorded printed books with evidence of provenance only when he came across them. They could not be harvested by a campaign of reading descriptive catalogues analogous to those that existed for manuscripts. It is now becoming possible to do that for incunabula, and the Material Evidence in Incunabula project led by Cristina Dondi will in time gather the evidence.[12] But it remains difficult to track provenance for books printed between 1500 and 1540. The advanced search in *MLGB*3 allows one to select printed books, but one cannot view all 482 of them presently there in order of date: it will sort by provenance and date. It is certain that further work on *in situ* collections, in cathedrals and in the university colleges, will increase the number of printed books substantially.

Before delving further into the challenge of using *MLGB* it will be necessary to review some numbers. As has been mentioned, Roger Mynors at a very early stage referred to the project as an index of monastic books, relevant to cross-matching with copies recorded from monastic libraries by the Grey Friars of Oxford in *Registrum Anglie*, but overlooking the fact that the friars reported on titles from six of the secular cathedrals as well as from those cathedrals with a monastic community. Indeed from Exeter, London and Salisbury they reported more than one hundred titles in each case. *MLGB* has been cited as evidence for the survival of some 5,000 books from the dissolved monasteries, but it pays to look more closely at the figures.

The very basic numbers organized by class and religious order are shown in TABLE 1. There are 6,726 books reported under the headings of 595 institutions. (It is difficult to allow for those books entered under two institutions, as should have happened with Easton's *Policraticus*, but they are not so numerous as to greatly disturb the figures. Not included in the count are some 140 institutions with other, normally documentary, evidence for a library but no traced books.) Benedictine

TABLE 1 Numbers of surviving books in *MLGB*, arranged by class and religious order

		HOUSES	BOOKS	%
MONASTIC ORDERS				
Benedictine		127	3,508	52.1
Cluniac		11	44	0.65
Augustinian		107	666	9.9
Premonstratensian		23	58	0.86
Cistercian		77	431	6.4
Carthusian		10	110	1.6
Bridgettine		1	111	1.6
Other		13	42	0.62
	Subtotal	369	4,970	73.9
MENDICANT ORDERS				
Carmelites		10	39	0.58
Austin friars		12	67	0.99
Dominicans		35	111	1.6
Franciscans		47	229	3.4
Other		4	17	0.25
	Subtotal	108	463	6.9
SECULAR INSTITUTIONS				
Cathedrals		23	708	10.5
Secular colleges		35	251	3.7
Hospitals		22	42	0.62
Other		11	32	0.47
	Subtotal	91	1,033	15.4
UNIVERSITIES				
University		2	26	0.39
Colleges and halls		25	234	3.5
	Subtotal	27	260	3.9
Total		595	6,726	100

TABLE 2 Percentage totals adjusted to account for medieval books still *in situ* in Oxford and Cambridge colleges

		HOUSES	OLD BOOKS	NEW BOOKS	% OF OLD	% OF NEW
MONASTIC ORDERS						
	Subtotal	369	4,970		73.9	57.6
MENDICANT ORDERS						
	Subtotal	108	463		6.9	5.4
SECULAR INSTITUTIONS						
	Subtotal	91	1,033		15.4	12.0
UNIVERSITIES						
University		2	26		0.39	
Colleges and halls		29	234	2,134	3.5	
	Subtotal	27	260	2,160	3.9	25.0
Total		595	6,726	8,626	100	100

abbeys and priories dominate with books recorded from 127 houses, of which 102 are men's houses and 25 women's houses. These women's houses account for 66 books out of the 3,500 from Benedictine houses, which include most of the largest collections of surviving books. Over 50 per cent of the total books in *MLGB* were from Benedictine houses on these figures. Augustinian canons and Cistercian monks account for some hundreds, and so do the secular cathedrals, of which Salisbury, Exeter, Hereford and Lincoln are well represented. On the big percentages here, monastic houses account for three-quarters of the recorded provenanceable survivors, secular institutions for 15 per cent, with the remaining 10 per cent divided between the mendicants and the universities.

These data display the state of knowledge as represented in *MLGB2*. Now, there has been a very significant impact on the numbers from the incorporation in *MLGB3* of medieval books that belonged to Oxford and Cambridge colleges in the Middle Ages (as separate from the medieval books they have acquired since). Some 1,900 books have been added for colleges and halls, so that the new figures look rather different. The new data for the universities and the changed percentage subtotals for other classes are shown in TABLE 2. While twenty-four colleges appeared in *MLGB2* because of provenanceable books that now survive outside their medieval colleges, the number rises to twenty-eight when books still in their medieval institutions are included. (The number 29 in the table includes King's College in Aberdeen: I have not attempted to exclude Scottish figures from *MLGB*, which takes a British view.) University books as a proportion of the surviving provenanceable books have risen in this count from just under 4 per cent to 25 per cent. The proportion represented by books from other types of institution has therefore fallen, though monastic books are still 58 per cent of the total.

Institutions represented by substantial numbers inevitably draw the attention, offering the promise of a collection much more open to study and understanding. Out of the 595 institutions included only 15 are at present represented by more than one hundred provenanced survivors. At this point should be interpolated the all-important comment: let no one imagine that *MLGB* records all the books surviving from any particular house. It can only record those that carry evidence of their medieval homes. How many surviving medieval books with no evidence of provenance – as interpreted to date – belonged to institutions, we have no means of knowing. We may guess that institutions with large numbers of recognized survivors were better at marking their property – and so register good evidence – than those with few now recognized, but that is only a guess.

All books surviving today have to have some route of preservation, but the houses that are represented by substantial numbers of surviving books have usually benefited from some form of group survival. Big numbers may more certainly reflect better chances of preservation than better evidence of provenance, and it is certainly dangerous to treat numbers of recognized books as in any way a proxy for the size of a medieval library. If 15 institutions are represented by a hundred books or more, then 580 are represented by fewer, and the fact is that 100 institutions as currently listed are represented by ten or more books, and 495 by fewer than ten. In handling a distribution model such as that in FIGURE 2, we must be aware that a very high proportion of the dots stand for very small numbers of books: 47 institutions are represented by three books, 95 by just two books, and 225 institutions by a single book. If one pictures the graph, the projected line may suggest a still larger number of houses represented by none.

Working out how one may extrapolate from a handful of books to some perception of the collection they represent is one way to move from such data towards the history of a library. Even in isolation the presence of a shelfmark is still evidence of a collection, an *ex libris* reflects some management, and a more elaborate note may do more, but I have not studied the evidence sufficiently to tell from how many one-book institutions one has the option to construct an edifice. The documentary evidence, discussed in Chapter 2, will help, since it is sometimes available from institutions with few if any survivors, but for many houses there is little indeed to go on.

On the other hand, the large collections of surviving books present many tempting avenues for inquiry. Fifteen libraries represent 2.5 per cent of the libraries but supplied nearly 60 per cent of the books recorded by Ker (TABLE 3). The top five (under 1 per cent of houses) supplied 1,917 books (29 per cent of books), three of them Benedictine cathedrals and two major abbeys. With more than 600 surviving books

TABLE 3 Ranking of religious houses by number of surviving books, showing percentages of the total number in *MLGB*

PLACE	SPECIES	NO.	%
Durham, Benedictine cathedral priory of St Cuthbert	OSB	612	9.1
Worcester, Benedictine cathedral priory of St Mary the Virgin	OSB	379	5.6
Canterbury, Benedictine cathedral priory of Holy Trinity or Christ Church	OSB	361	5.4
Canterbury, Benedictine abbey of St Augustine	OSB	295	4.4
Bury St Edmunds, Benedictine abbey of St Edmund, King and Martyr	OSB	271	4.0
Salisbury, cathedral church of St Mary the Virgin	cath	217	3.7
Llanthony Secunda, Augustinian priory of St Mary the Virgin and St John the Baptist	OSA	166	2.9
St Albans, Benedictine abbey of St Alban	OSB	153	2.7
Rochester, Benedictine cathedral priory of St Andrew	OSB	152	2.7
Exeter, cathedral church of St Peter	cath	151	2.7
Reading, Benedictine abbey of Saint Mary the Virgin	OSB	131	2.3
Hereford, cathedral church of St Ethelbert	cath	126	2.2
Norwich, Benedictine cathedral priory of Holy Trinity	OSB	126	2.2
Syon, Middlesex, Bridgettine abbey of St Saviour, St Mary the Virgin, and St Bridget	OSS	111	1.9
Lincoln, cathedral church of St Mary the Virgin	cath	103	1.8
Total		3,353	58.5

TABLE 4 The same ranking, with the inclusion of five university colleges that keep books known to have been in their possession before 1540

PLACE	SPECIES	NO.	%
Durham, Benedictine cathedral priory of St Cuthbert	OSB	612	9.1
Worcester, Benedictine cathedral priory of St Mary the Virgin	OSB	379	5.6
Canterbury, Benedictine cathedral priory of Holy Trinity or Christ Church	OSB	361	5.4
Oxford, Merton College		344	
Oxford, Balliol College		313	
Canterbury, Benedictine abbey of St Augustine	OSB	295	4.4
Bury St Edmunds, Benedictine abbey of St Edmund, King and Martyr	OSB	271	4.0
Cambridge, Peterhouse		258	
Salisbury, cathedral church of St Mary the Virgin	cath	217	3.7
Llanthony Secunda, Augustinian priory of St Mary the Virgin and St John the Baptist	OSA	166	2.9
St Albans, Benedictine abbey of St Alban	OSB	153	2.7
Rochester, Benedictine cathedral priory of St Andrew	OSB	152	2.7
Exeter, cathedral church of St Peter	cath	151	2.7
Cambridge, Gonville Hall		135	
Reading, Benedictine abbey of Saint Mary the Virgin	OSB	131	2.3
Hereford, cathedral church of St Ethelbert	cath	126	2.2
Norwich, Benedictine cathedral priory of Holy Trinity	OSB	126	2.2
Cambridge, Pembroke College		119	
Syon, Middlesex, Bridgettine abbey of St Saviour, St Mary the Virgin, and St Bridget	OSS	111	1.9
Lincoln, cathedral church of St Mary the Virgin	cath	103	1.8
Oxford, Magdalen College		101	
Total excluding colleges		3,353	58.5
Total including colleges		4,623	53.5

recognized to date, Durham is certainly the best-preserved medieval collection by number from the Middle Ages. It may well be the best preserved as a proportion of its original holdings: 600 books of all periods compared with a principal stock of some 900 in 1395 looks impressive next to (say) Canterbury cathedral, from where 360 books of all periods is still a high rate of preservation when compared with a catalogue of 1,837 books in 1326.[13] We need to be careful in our language in such comparisons. We are including books now in existence that were made after the documents were drawn up: such books are not survivors from the catalogues but from the libraries, and we must hold this lack of chronological fit in our minds as an inevitable anomaly in our evidence. A majority of the manuscripts of Durham cathedral priory remain in the cathedral's library today, now managed by the University Library. Many, but not a majority, of the manuscripts from Worcester remain at Worcester, but more were there in the early seventeenth century, when listed by Patrick Young in 1622.[14] Otherwise documentary evidence from Worcester is severely limited. Canterbury cathedral priory and St Augustine's abbey in Canterbury benefited from the interest of manuscript collectors in the sixteenth century, and in the case of the cathedral it was deans and archbishops who had the interest to preserve many of the surviving books.[15] In an important lecture from 1941, Ker showed the differential rates of survival of different types of book by comparing the books with evidence of provenance against the large medieval catalogues that survive from both institutions.[16] His work drew attention to the marked preference of sixteenth-century collectors for large, handsome, well-made books of the twelfth century containing works of the Latin Fathers. These, he showed, had survived much better than works of thirteenth- or early-fourteenth-century scholastics, which had lost their interest by the sixteenth century. Other explanations may operate in other contexts, but one must always bear in mind that the preservation of large groups of manuscripts, or indeed of printed books, may be conditioned by preferences four hundred years ago that may not be apparent to us.

The new data from the university colleges alter this reckoning again. The entry of two Oxford colleges and three Cambridge colleges which have retained more that one hundred of their medieval manuscripts is shown in TABLE 4. The new reckoning is not yet complete: New College and Lincoln College will probably also need to be added to this table in due course, but their books have not yet been examined to determine which were owned before 1540.

Including the university colleges, the top twenty are either Benedictine or secular foundations, with the two exceptions being Llanthony Secunda, a priory of Augustinian canons near Gloucester, and the early-fifteenth-century foundation Syon Abbey, of the Order of the Holy Saviour, in Middlesex. Llanthony with 166 has the largest tally from any Augustinian house, and from here also survives a fourteenth-century catalogue with 400 entries. *Ex libris* are inconsistently found, but a large proportion of the survivors have come down to us together as a collection in Lambeth Palace Library. The next largest tally from an Augustinian house is 40 from Cirencester. From Syon Abbey we have 111 identified survivors from a catalogue of around 1,400, of which only half a dozen carry an *ex libris* and even fewer the shelfmarks that are very prominent in structuring the important early-sixteenth-century catalogue of this library, superbly edited by Vincent Gillespie. Syon is an example where the identification of books depends quite heavily on the evidence of the documentary record.

The highest number of books known from other religious orders is generally much lower. A tally of twenty or thirty books appears quite substantial, but next to the major collections it is not easy to build rich interpretations. The largest number from any Cistercian house is 54 from Buildwas in Shropshire, and the story of their survival is a complicated one because Buildwas was deaccessioning books in the early fifteenth century. Three Yorkshire houses follow in the ranking, Fountains with 42, Byland with 27 and Rievaulx with 22. Numbers of books from the convents of friars are small, the largest number being 36 from the Austin friars in Cambridge. The library in their convent in York is represented now by ten survivors, but we have the catalogue showing more than three hundred books in 1372, a collection that would more than double in size within twenty years with the accession, shown as additions in the catalogue, of 340 books that belonged to Friar John Argam, the largest private collection documented for us from medieval England.[17] That such a library was winnowed away over the last century and a half of the friary's existence and the five hundred years since is clear evidence that we should not rush to treat low survival numbers as implying a small collection. In numbers, what makes the difference between Llanthony with 400 books in its catalogue of around 1360 and its 166 known survivors and these York friars with 600 books around 1390 and 10 recognized survivors is explained by the opportunity of preservation.[18]

When we look at books from nunneries, we find that in aggregate there are 109 books recognized from forty-one different houses, on average little more than two per house and most often just one. Best preserved in number are the 16 books from Barking abbey (Essex). The earliest of these is a gospel book of the early eleventh century, now Oxford, Bodleian Library, MS. Bodl. 155, owned in the sixteenth century by Stephen Batman, Archbishop Parker's chaplain, who helped in the collection of Parker's famous library.[19] The others include a higher proportion of late medieval books in French and English than is usual in *MLGB*, but some of the earlier Latin books share the same long *ex libris* inscription, entered by a librarian in the thirteenth century, organizing the library. She was presumably the nun referred to as *libraria* in the custumal of the abbey (known to us from a copy made for Abbess Sybil in 1404), which describes the procedure at the

Lenten election in terms very similar to what we find in the custumals of Westminster abbey (1266) and St Augustine's abbey (*c.* 1340).[20] That connexion through the custumals is a warning not to take sixteen survivors from Barking as evidence that the abbey did not have an organized library for the nuns. The custumal affirms the Benedictine practice of reading. By contrast, from the Franciscan nunnery in Stamford we have identified only a copy of the *Rule of Seynt Benet* (in English), printed in London in 1517, which belonged to the prioress Dame Margaret Stanburne (now Oxford, Bodleian Library, Arch. A.d.15), which leaves us entirely in ignorance of the conventual books.

Faced with some 595 lists of books, most of them very short, one has to have principles for interpreting them, and Ker was of a generation that did not set out an interpretation in headnotes. He left it to us to learn the ropes, though his introduction is wonderfully clear on his thinking, particularly about the evidence for provenance, which is sometimes local and sometimes complex.

A book can only be recognized if it carries evidence, and a book can only be entered if it survives. Those are two preconditions that many books from institutions may not have met. We rarely know that the older books were still in place when the later ones were acquired. One would like to get a more general profile by counting the 6,728 or 8,628 books by period in this way. But this is very difficult. Electronic presentation does not do well at sorting Roman numerals qualified by obliques, dashes and fractions, and translating all palaeographical datings into surrogate Arabic numerals forces one to review thousands of judgements. Resolving numbers into a bar chart by century produces a fairly uninformative result. One sees relatively small numbers from the centuries before 1100, a great bulge in the twelfth century, a drop in the thirteenth century, and a substantial rise in the fourteenth and fifteenth centuries. With more experience of medieval library catalogues than of statistics from actual books, the dip in the thirteenth century was less than I had expected, but none the less I look on these numbers as unhelpful. I do not think *MLGB*3 will provide a general statistical resource.[21]

But we should concentrate on the things to look out for when thinking about individual libraries. First, *ex libris*, especially uniform ones that reflect an active librarian and which may, indeed, provide a date horizon for provenanceability. A librarian at Reading abbey (Berks.) in the Middle Ages entered *ex libris* in the books around 1250 and none of his successors did. Later books from Reading may not be recognized.[22] Signs of active librarianship, even if it is only once in the Middle Ages, are always a positive indicator.[23] Deciding whether they are continual, fitful or occasional activity is a necessary part of the interpretation. Pressmarks of whatever kind must be a good indicator of a library, and notes on contents at the front of a book very likely reflect the drafting of a catalogue. At Bury St Edmunds (Suff.) we have a librarian in the 1350s and 1360s who not only wrote detailed accounts of the contents, with biographies of the authors, at the front of the books, but also compiled them into a bibliography of church authors.[24] Attempting to interpret survivors in chronological terms, however, is very difficult, but it is worth sorting the results that way just in case an obvious anomaly emerges in a particular library.

MLGB brings together individual books, more or sometimes less plausibly, under an institutional heading. There is rejoicing when a book is added whose provenance is newly recognized, as another brick in the wall, and especially if it brings evidence for an institution hitherto absent; it also often helps in our use of a particular book to know where it was owned and used.[25] But no entry in *MLGB* represents a library in any meaningful sense at any point in its existence. For that we must turn to medieval library catalogues, which offer a snapshot of a collection of books at a certain moment.

TWO

English Medieval Library Catalogues

READING MEDIEVAL LIBRARY CATALOGUES is the best way to learn about the holdings and organization of medieval libraries. This was first properly recognized in England in the 1830s. In 1831 the antiquary Joseph Hunter, a Yorkshireman from the West Riding who started his career as a cutler, had printed the 1555 post-dissolution booklist from Monk Bretton priory alongside notes on other monastic libraries, including an indenture recording the loan of nineteen books from Hinton Charterhouse.[26] In 1838 Beriah Botfield in the Surtees Society published many of the medieval catalogues and other library records of Durham cathedral priory.[27] This interest in the 1830s represented a healthy change. A generation earlier was still in the Age of Lead for medieval studies in Britain. In 1795 the antiquary John Nichols commented on the late-fifteenth-century Leicester abbey library catalogue by William Charite, MS. Laud Misc. 623, with its double listing: 'Many books are referred to some other arrangement; many have only 2 folia. The first words of some are given; and, after all our enquiries, many of the writers here enumerated must remain as unknown as they are uninteresting; and perhaps posterity has very little reason to regret the loss of the Library of Leicester abbey.'[28]

The revival of medieval studies from the 1840s and 1850s onwards saw contributions to medieval library history in England, but it was in the years between about 1895 and 1925 that M.R. James and Mary Bateson brought out editions of most of the major catalogues.[29] These editions sought to cross-match catalogue entries with surviving books, but they made no attempt to identify the works that the medieval books contained, works that might include classical and patristic books as well as writings of any period in the Middle Ages, down to the date of the catalogue itself. How far this lack of identifications arose from believing that readers could recognize the titles that appeared in medieval catalogues one cannot say. I harbour a suspicion that they knew how difficult it can be to recognize all the works that appear but preferred to hide behind a pretence of common knowledge. Let me not press the point, but some 8,000 different works have turned up in the medieval library records from England, and those of us who have worked on the Corpus of British Medieval Library Catalogues have had a long learning curve in recognizing some of these works. Some identifications are difficult but not impossible, some become possible only as one joins up second, third and fourth occurrences of a title, each bringing a little bit of extra information. For stable reference to texts by author or title is not a given in the Middle Ages. Identities might be changed in the process of transmission, a textual process that can be understood and reversed.[30]

The Corpus set out to annotate line by line: the more experienced reader with these volumes will make more rapid progress through a catalogue because the experienced reader does not need to read the interlined notes, skipping over what is familiar. But for the newer recruit to the subject the information to help make sense of the document is there as it is read. There should always be the notes to allow some level of comprehension entry by entry. After all, who is to decide what is a sufficiently straightforward author or work not to need annotation? And the headnotes to each library make a concise attempt to draw together what can be learnt from the evidence available for the development of each collection represented. Writing such headnotes is an exercise in research and interpretation, piecing the evidence together in relation to what is known about a library, its books and the institution that owned it. Working through the evidence for this or that library, be it rich or meagre, is straightforward. The larger question is how to extrapolate from the particular to fill the gaps in the evidence and see the larger picture of libraries as such and their place in the book economy.

Before turning to that question, it will be necessary to introduce the repertory for this class of evidence, the Corpus of British Medieval Library Catalogues. Sixteen volumes in this series have been published at the time of writing, some of them in more than one physical volume. A page count so far is just over 12,000 pages plus another 1,200 pages of introductions. The principle is to publish catalogues, booklists or other records that bear witness to the *library* of an institution. We have found no lists of bursary books, although registers are included in a few catalogues.[31] In most cases lists that mention only service books are excluded. During work on the secular institutions – the cathedrals of Old Foundation, collegiate churches and hospitals – the avoidance of service books was relaxed as it was considered (incorrectly) that the colleges and hospitals would have little else to show. So the volume on secular cathedrals includes the richly detailed thirteenth-century descriptions of the service books at St Paul's cathedral, for example, though we have no substantial medieval library catalogue from there, despite the cathedral's having had an important library.[32] For the Corpus a 'list' is in the first instance required to have two entries. Principles as to the genre of record and the desire to enter whatever will usefully contribute to the eventual index as a key to knowledge have sometimes pulled in contrary directions.

Rather than follow the practice of the German and Swiss series Mittelalterliche Bibliothekskataloge Deutschlands und der Schweiz, which is organized by diocese, the British Corpus is organized mainly by institutional categories. There is a volume on the libraries of the Augustinian canons, another that combines but does not merge the libraries of Cistercian monks with those of Gilbertine canons and Premonstratensian canons. Benedictine monks occupy several volumes, including several devoted to large catalogues. The two universities each have volumes, and there are volumes on the secular colleges, among them Eton and Winchester.[33] There is here an underlying view that it makes more sense to treat Cistercians all together than it does to treat, say, the abbeys, convents and colleges of Lincoln or London diocese as a local group. Scotland, on the other hand, was treated geographically, and two volumes are devoted to works of a different nature. *Registrum Anglie* has been mentioned and will be discussed in what follows: this is the Franciscan union catalogue, edited as the second volume of the series and quite challenging to use. The other is Henry de Kirkestede's bibliographical essay on more than six hundred church authors, which used *Registrum Anglie* as its major source although without adding very much by way of locations.[34] Henry (d. after 8 April 1378) was the librarian and later prior of Bury St Edmunds; his book is a valuable witness to perceptions of church authors and their works, but it brings little grist to the mill of copies in particular libraries. It does add some confusion in the form of entries which he derived from learned sources for works already lost when Jerome was drawing up his catalogue of Christian writers.[35] A special indexing symbol was needed for such empty records. Still to appear in the Corpus are the volumes on the cathedral priories of Canterbury and of Durham, both of them including important documents, and a new edition to replace the first volume of the series from 1990, *The Friars' Libraries*, as well as a printed cumulative index. This final volume of cumulative indexes to the series will have as its core the 'List of Identifications', available online since 2003, but also accessible by Author/Title search in *MLGB3*. Based on the documents but signalling where these can be controlled by the extant copies described in the record, this gives a fuller and truer sense than has hitherto been available of what works existed in British libraries, in what numbers. It allows one to see what works were available widely or sparsely or in a particular setting. The List of Identifications was originally intended to provide contributors to the series with identification notes for works already encountered in a stabilized form, to ensure consistency and accuracy. As more documents have been edited, the accumulation of evidence sometimes corrected identifications, so that this cumulative index should be the starting point for a reader wanting to know about the frequency with which particular titles are found.

Across the twenty-one volumes that will be printed and annotated there are what appear to be 1,200 documents. As a count of documents, that number must be reduced to about 1,000 because it counts many times over a few documents that happen to report books in many institutions, documents which are usually broken up in the Corpus to be treated as evidence for each institution separately. Two of these documents represent short tours in England, one by a well-connected Italian in the circle of Pope Paul II, perhaps around 1526, and another by an unknown agent of Henry VIII in Lincolnshire in 1528, reporting between them on fifty libraries.[36] The antiquary John Leland (*c.* 1503–1552) provided reports on mostly rare titles from some 120 institutions between 1533 and 1535.[37] There are also some wills that bequeath books to more than one institution, and their treatment depends on whether or not the institutions in question are all in the same volume of the Corpus or across several.

The documents can be categorized by function, as catalogues in a broad sense, inventories, location lists for parts of a collection, lists that reflect accession or loss or expenditure. For present purposes I am concerned only with those that seek to reflect the entire contents of a library at a particular time. Even here one can speak of typological variation in catalogues, much of which reflects the period when a catalogue was drawn up.[38] Early lists tend to survive because they were written into the back or front of books, and it was the books that have been preserved and the lists survive by chance. Later there are lists kept as records on parchment rolls, and catalogues that are themselves the size of books. Early ones were simple booklists, sometimes itemizing the contents of books, but not always making it clear where a list of contents from one book ends and another begins. By the twelfth century there are often catalogues that will name the first or principal work as the identifier of the book and then add a note of contents, *in quo continentur*, before a listing of the works. Such contents lists would have been entered at the front of the volumes in question, very likely in preparation for making the catalogue, though their existence would also help a reader of the book. The regular existence of contents lists in books from one institution, when encountered in *MLGB*, is probably evidence that a catalogue was made, even if we no longer have it. No attempt has been made to count such potentially inferable catalogues. One document, a substantial fourteenth-century catalogue from Peterborough abbey (BP21), very strangely has a consistent practice of omitting to mention the first work from any book that contained more than one: that much can be shown when cross-matching catalogue and survivors.[39] The explanation is likely to be that the compiler began to copy from contents lists at just some such indicator as *in quo continentur*, ignoring the primary work. In a book of only a single work, there would be only one title to copy. It is evidence that it is a secondary

FIGURE 4 The *Prima Pars* of John Whitfield's catalogue of the library at St Martin's priory, Dover, 1389 (Oxford, Bodleian Library, MS. Bodl. 920, fol. 18r)

Ordo locacionis	Nomina voluminum	Locus probacionis	Dicciones probacionum	Summa foliorum	Numerus quaternorum
·i· I	IIII			I	
1	Doctrinale magnum J. p[rim]e	4	est diminutiua	149	1
2	Doctrinale mag[ist]ri Willi p[rim]e	2	has tres d. c. t.	163	7
3	Liber urbani	3	t[em]pe rudimentu[m]	216	11
4	Doctrinale mag[ist]ri J. de douor	3	cu[m] translat[a]e	143	4
5	Doctrinale mag[ist]ri cu[m] plur[ibus]	7	es longa mutta	184	9
6	Donatus glosatus	5	sol vel luna	156	8
7	Lib[er] catonis & ch[ri]sti[ani] p[rim]e	6	redibit morta	101	10
8	Cato glosat[us] gallice	3	aucup[ar]i i uri	162	7
9	Alexandri monachor[um]	3	ammenus exposi	93	3
10	Lucanus	2	crassus erat	79	1
11	Glose lucani	2	gentes effunder[e]	142	7
12	Ouidi[us] metamorfosios	3	cesserunt uici	178	1
13	Liber de iiii partibus gramatice	3	d. c. d. g.		
14	Liber grecismi	2	est quie		

Musci expositum corpus nudato gerenti
Lacti commixto mellisque liquore perunctum
Tactu cupido mirabilis agmine linquit
Si lapidem tulerit facto grege spicula figens
Vibrataque cutem fugiet per vulnera mille

DE IASPIDE

Iaspidis esse decem species septemque feruntur
Hic et multorum cognoscitur esse colorum
Et multis nasci perhibetur partibus orbis
Optimus in viridi translucentique colore
Et qui plus soleat virtutis habere probatur
Caste gestatus fugat et febrem et ydropem
Appositusque iuvat mulierem parturientem
Et tutamentum portanti creditur esse
Nam consecratus gratum facit atque potentem
Et sicut perhibent fantasmata noxia pellit
Cuius in argento vis fortior esse putatur.

DE SAPHIRO

Saphiri species digitis aptissima regum
Egregium fulgens puroque simillima celo
Vilior est nullo virtutibus atque decore
Hic et sirtites lapis a plerisque vocatur
Quem circa sirtes libicis pervenit harenis
Fluctibus expulsus fervente freto reperitur
Ille sed optimus est quem tellus medica gignit
Qui tamen asseritur numquam transmittere visum

f. IIII

lapidarius medicus ... Muscis expositum corpus ... 23 ... 3.

catalogue, copied, with this measure of incompetence, from an earlier catalogue and copied by someone other than the keeper of the books.

Oxford, Bodleian Library, MS. Bodl. 920 is the catalogue of St Martin's priory at Dover, a small house dependent on Canterbury cathedral priory (BM1). Its catalogue, drawn up by Br. John Whitfield in 1389, is a fine example of the librarian's craft and one of several representatives of a fourteenth-century golden age for catalogues. It is in three parts. The first, acting as an inventory for the custodian, is in shelfmark order with one line for each book, including the *secundo folio*, the arbitrary identifier, the first words on the start of the second leaf, that identifies a manuscript as object (FIGURE 4).[40] In a handful of cases we can match survivors to the catalogue. They show, as Whitfield explained in the preface to his catalogue, that the part-one entry also appears in the lower margin of the book to which it refers on the second folio or any other folio if the *dicta probatoria* have been taken from the third, fourth, fifth leaf (FIGURE 5). The second part of the catalogue goes through the collection again in the same sequence, this time using as many lines as were needed to list the contents, including the opening words of each work contained. This part was intended for the dedicated library user who wanted to browse the catalogue. The third part was an index for the brisk library user who wanted to find a work more quickly. Whitfield's inclusion of opening words, *incipits* as we call them in the craft – or should I say mystery? – of identifying medieval works, is very useful to the Corpus as a whole, because with obscure titles it provides a means to search for the text unfettered by the variation of titles, and an identification secured from the *incipit* at Dover can be exported to help identify copies of the same obscure

FIGURE 5 A leaf from a Dover manuscript showing John Whitfield's marks at the foot, corresponding to the entry in his catalogue at J.IIII.9 (Oxford, Bodleian Library, MS. Digby 13, fol. 3r)

title in other booklists. In the cumulative list, the occurrence of 'inc.' in brackets after an index entry stands for *incipit* and it shows that the identification is based on real evidence.

From the thousand-plus documents edited in the Corpus the number of entries annotated is currently 50,242. About 38,000 of those amount to identifications that can be indexed under author and title in the List of Identifications. The others may be generic titles such as gospels and epistles, missals and breviaries, or anonymous and unidentifiable titles, perhaps the equivalent of trade books, or works too loosely described to be interpretable: a book of medicine, a book of law. All of these are none the less indexed generically in the individual volumes, and how far a cumulative generic index will be possible will be a decision for the end of the series.

The overall pattern is that there are more later records than earlier. In fact the numbers rise steeply. There are 10 very limited documents from before 1100. There are 28 from the twelfth century, some of them quite substantial. From the thirteenth century the number of records rises to 54, but some of these are short lists of gifts or other accessions, or equally short reports of loans and losses, rather than catalogues describing whole collections. Such subsidiary documents become much more common as time goes on. From the fourteenth century the number of documents is 190. From the fifteenth century the number is 420. If one were to provide average numbers of entries per document by century, there would be a steep decline as the number of lists mentioning five, four, three, two books becomes a bigger share of the documents that exist. We are collecting documents that individually tell us less about the libraries. The focus shifts from catalogues to lists of books given or bequeathed at a particular time. The steep increase in the number of records may reflect several factors. One is the increased importance of secular institutions, with preservation boosted by the fact that university colleges and secular cathedrals have had uninterrupted histories and can retain substantial archives. Archive-keeping from the fourteenth century onwards is usually less selective than from an earlier period. And the secular institutions were more likely to receive documented gifts than religious houses, whose gifts of books more likely came undocumented from within their communities. It becomes very important to tune into the developing character of the record evidence and the changing shape of the library culture that it reflects as a precursor to trying to interpret the great number of these documents.

In this welter of documentary evidence, even one document can make a great difference. Among the relatively thin records from the beginning of the fourteenth century, and among the even thinner evidence for the holdings of Cistercian libraries, there is a list of books bailed into the hands of the abbot and convent of Bordesley abbey in Worcestershire by Guy de Beauchamp, earl of Warwick, on 1 May 1306 (Z2). It survives only as a transcript made in 1689, but it describes twenty-seven volumes of French romances, and there is no better testimony to a private aristocratic collection of such books.[41] The deed commits the books to the abbey to remain indefinitely, and there is nothing to suggest that this was merely a short-term bailment. What it says about the reading habits of the monks of Bordesley is quite another matter. Why this transfer? Why this record? Earl Guy died in 1315 and was buried at Bordesley.

It is the high-end libraries for which the best evidence survives. *MLGB2* has fifteen institutions with more than one hundred recognized books surviving, and another eighy-five with ten or more books, leaving close to five hundred institutions with fewer than ten books now recognized. The evidence of catalogues is much fuller. A list of forty or fifty books can feel quite substantial when one is studying it, and there are more than two hundred lists with upwards of fifty entries. The biggest of these catalogues listed by size, those with more than 350 entries, are shown in TABLE 5. Among these 24 at the top of

TABLE 5 The largest extant catalogues arranged by size

PLACE	SPECIES	CBMLC REFERENCE	DOCUMENT TYPE
Canterbury St Augustine's	OSB	BA1	catalogue
Canterbury Christ Church	OSB	BC005	catalogue
Syon	OSS	SS1	catalogue
Leicester	OSA	A20	catalogue
York St Mary's	OSB	B120	catalogue
York Austin Friars	OESA	F56	catalogue
Ramsey	OSB	B068	catalogue
Exeter	cath	SC033	inventory
Durham	OSB	BD011	catalogue
Llanthony	OSA	A16	catalogue
Oxford All Souls	coll	UO007	inventory
Oxford New College	coll	UO070	inventory
Oxford Merton	coll	UO068	inventory
Durham	OSB	BD005	catalogue
Cambridge Peterhouse	coll	UC048	catalogue
Dover	OSB	BM1	catalogue
Oxford Merton	coll	UO066	borrowers
Glastonbury	OSB	B039	catalogue
Durham	OSB	BD012	catalogue
Oxford All Souls	coll	UO016	inventory
Oxford All Souls	coll	UO006	inventory
Meaux	OCist	Z14	catalogue
Saint Albans	OSB	R (15)	select list

DESCRIPTION	DATE	NO. OF ENTRIES
Catalogue of the library, late 14th cent, continued to late 15th cent.	1380	1,837
Catalogue of the library, 1326	1326	1,831
Catalogue of the library by Thomas Betson, *c.* 1500, with additions, *c.* 1524	1524	1,464
Catalogue of books, 1463, 1477 × 1494	1490	941
Index catalogue of selected authors, 15th cent.	1440	653
Catalogue of the library, 1372, with additions	1372	646
Fragment of a catalogue of books, mid-14th cent.	1350	609
Inventory of goods, 6 September 1506	1506	585
Catalogue of books in the Spendement, 1392 onwards	1392	516
Catalogue of the library, *c.* 1355–1360	1360	508
Inventory of books in the library, *c.* 1443	1443	480
Inventory of the library, *c.* 1415	1415	466
Inventory for the Marian Commissioners, 1556	1556	457
Catalogue of the library, mid-12th cent.	1160	456
Catalogue, 24 December 1418	1418	456
John Whitfield's catalogue of the library, 1389	1389	450
Theology books in the annual *electio*, 8 December 1519	1519	442
Catalogue of the library, 1247/8, with additions	1248	402
Catalogue of books in the Cloister, 1395	1395	386
Inventory of books in the library, *c.* 1513	1513	384
Inventory of books in the library, *c.* 1443	1443	369
Catalogue of books, 1396	1396	363
Registrum Anglie	1290	362

TABLE 6 The largest extant catalogues arranged by date

PLACE	SPECIES	CBMLC REFERENCE	DOCUMENT TYPE
Durham	OSB	BD5	catalogue
Glastonbury	OSB	B39	catalogue
Saint Albans	OSB	R (15)	select list
Canterbury Christ Church	OSB	BC5	catalogue
Ramsey	OSB	B68	catalogue
Llanthony	OSA	A16	catalogue
York Austin Friars	OESA	F56	catalogue
Canterbury St Augustine	OSB	BA1	catalogue
Dover	OSB	BM1	catalogue
Durham	OSB	BD11	catalogue
Durham	OSB	BD12	catalogue
Meaux	OCist	Z14	catalogue
Oxford New College	coll	UO70	inventory
Cambridge Peterhouse	coll	UC48	catalogue
York St Mary's	OSB	B120	catalogue
Oxford All Souls	coll	UO7	inventory
Oxford All Souls	coll	UO6	inventory
Leicester	OSA	A20	catalogue
Syon	OSS	SS1	catalogue
Exeter	cath	SC033	inventory
Oxford All Souls	coll	UO016	inventory
Oxford Merton	coll	UO066	borrowers
Oxford Merton	coll	UO068	inventory

DESCRIPTION	DATE	NO. OF ENTRIES	
Catalogue of the library, mid-12th cent.	1160	456	
Catalogue of the library, 1247/8, with additions	1248	402	
Registrum Anglie	1290	362	
Catalogue of the library, 1326	1326	1,831	
Fragment of a catalogue of books, mid-14th cent.	1350	609	
Catalogue of the library, *c.* 1355–1360	1360	508	
Catalogue of the library, 1372, with additions	1372	646	
Catalogue of the library, late 14th cent, continued to late 15th cent.	1380	1,837	
John Whitfield's catalogue of the library, 1389	1389	450	
Catalogue of books in the Spendement, 1392 onwards	1392	516	902
Catalogue of books in the Cloister, 1395	1395	386	
Catalogue of books, 1396	1396	363	
Inventory of the library, *c.* 1415	1415	466	
Catalogue, 24 December 1418	1418	456	
Index catalogue of selected authors, 15th cent.	1440	653	
Inventory of books in the library, *c.* 1443	1443	480	849
Inventory of books in the library, *c.* 1443	1443	369	
Catalogue of books, 1463, 1477 × 1494	1490	941	
Catalogue of the library by Thomas Betson, *c.* 1500, with additions, *c.* 1524	1500	1,464	
Inventory of goods, 6 September 1506	1506	585	
Inventory of books in the library, *c.* 1513	1513	384	
Theology books in the annual *electio*, 8 December 1519	1519	442	
Inventory for the Marian Commissioners, 1556	1556	457	

the scale, there are ten Benedictine catalogues, two Augustinian, one Cistercian and one Bridgettine. Exeter cathedral is the only secular church to appear, on the strength of an inventory dated 1506 (SC35), and the comparative evidence suggests that Exeter cathedral library was indeed exceptional at this date in its collection of older books.[42] There are also seven university college lists here, and this is the normality which older editions of *MLGB* had belied, that university colleges were an important part of the late medieval library sector, and better knowable, by record and by survival, than most.

A change in perceptions is made possible when the same list is viewed in date order, in TABLE 6. From the twelfth century, there is only one big list, from Durham. Now, it cannot be said that Durham was the only library of this size in England in the middle of the twelfth century, but it does compare very favourably with Bury St Edmunds, which had a catalogue of some 261 entries in the third quarter of the twelfth century (B13). By the late fourteenth century Bury would have a library getting on for twice the size of that of Durham, so relative position on the scale of size is not stable. By aggregating two lists from Durham, those of the spendement (516) and the cloister (386) in 1392 and 1395, we have a total of just over 900 entries.[43] We have no list at all from Bury at this date, but Henry de Kirkestede used a system of class-marking by author and subject, A for Augustine and Ambrose, B for Bernard and Bible, and so on: by taking the highest numbers in each letter class as represented by recognized survivors, the total number of books at Bury under this system was not less than 2,100, and that is the biggest number we can project for any library in England.[44] (Of course one cannot set a date to that number as one does not know how long the system was continued at Bury after Henry's time.)

From the thirteenth century there is only Glastonbury (Som.) showing at around 400 entries in the middle of the century. The thirteenth century is a thin period, and it can only be wondered why evidence of this kind becomes scarcer in the thirteenth century than in the twelfth or the fourteenth. If it were a simple matter that thirteenth-century records had been superseded and discarded – which is plausible – then we need to consider why we have more from the twelfth century than from the thirteenth. Is the fact that some were copied into books sufficient answer on that point?

The fourth column of the table gives a categorization of the documents, and these very substantial lists are mostly described as 'catalogues'; that is, they seek to describe a whole collection in some detail, notwithstanding that earlier catalogues tend to have less detail than later ones. Catalogues were meant to serve library purposes, helping the keeper know what was in the collection, and by the fourteenth century at least also helping the potential reader. Inventories, on the other hand, are made to record and control property, so that the entry for a book will usually be a single line, identifying the book by one work only and the *secundo folio*. As a type of record these begin, in a very small way, in the late thirteenth century, but they become numerous in the fourteenth, fifteenth and sixteenth centuries.[45] In the Corpus as a whole, there are almost two hundred inventories, a few of them with more than 400 books, as seen in the table, but many with a mere handful of books, often in secular colleges where study was not a high priority.

In the table showing the largest records by size, St Albans (Herts.) appears as the least with 362 titles, classified as a 'select list' and coming from *Registrum Anglie*. It may be that such a select list of titles shrinks dramatically when considered as books. It is difficult to integrate the evidence of *Registrum* into the wider picture based on booklists. The document makes no attempt to describe books or their contents: rather, it is a list of works with a numerical union reference showing whether a particular place had reported holding a copy of that title. The big returns found in *Registrum* are shown in TABLE 7. More titles

TABLE 7 Houses in *Registrum Anglie* from which big returns were incorporated

PLACE	SPECIES	NO. OF ENTRIES
Saint Albans	OSB	362
Canterbury Christ Church	OSB	356
Woburn	OCist	248
Bury St Edmunds	OSB	246
Margam	OCist	242
Ford	OCist	240
Merton	OSA	231
Guisborough	OSA	184
Exeter	cath	168
Hexham	OSA	160
Newminster	OCist	159
Lewes	Cluniac	153
Salisbury	cath	146
London St Paul's cathedral	cath	135
Battle	OSB	128
York St Mary's abbey	OSB	123
Reading	OSB	114
Buildwas	OCist	112
Waltham	OSA	111
Crowland	OSB	110
Melrose	OCist	102
Cirencester	OSA	98

are reported from St Albans than from anywhere else, but there are twenty-one institutions visited by the friars who compiled *Registrum* with reports of more than one hundred titles. Some of these are places that have left us little other evidence of their books at all, places that should earn a headnote in *MLGB* even if there are no recognized survivors to record.

Reading down this table, which is in order of the size of report in *Registrum* towards the end of the thirteenth century, we are not well placed to judge the reports against other evidence. TABLE 8 therefore presents as a control measure the number of surviving books from these institutions which have been logged (*column 4*), entries in catalogues from some of these institutions (*column 5*), and an aggregate figure (*column 6*) which represents an attempt to use other evidence to gain a rough sense of the library over time (for Bury, for example, there is the evidence of the desk numbering, as we have seen, from which some total numbers may be derived). The catalogues, such as those for Canterbury and Bury, may seem to offer better evidence, but we must remember that the Bury catalogue here dates from more than one hundred years earlier than *Registrum* (though the patristic books of greatest interest to the compilers were very likely already in the library at Bury when the catalogue was drawn up), whereas the Canterbury catalogue dates from thirty or forty years later, while the catalogue from St Mary's in York dates from one hundred and fifty years later. Again its focus is on the Fathers, and it is possible that both *Registrum* and the York index-catalogue represent works of the Fathers in copies written in the twelfth century. We have not the means to know.

One case is particularly interesting. The list of 96 books from Crowland, an undatable document which survives at the back of a legal manuscript now in Berlin (B24), largely overlaps with the 110 titles in the *Registrum*. Mary and Richard Rouse argued very plausibly that it was a draft list made up by the friars at Crowland before framing

TABLE 8 Houses with big returns in *Registrum Anglie* aggregated with other evidence

PLACE	SPECIES
Saint Albans	OSB
Canterbury Christ Church	OSB
Woburn	OCist
Bury St Edmunds	OSB
Margam	OCist
Ford	OCist
Merton	OSA
Guisborough	OSA
Exeter	cath
Hexham	OSA
Newminster	OCist
Lewes	Cluniac
Salisbury	cath
London St Paul's cathedral	cath
Battle	OSB
York St Mary's abbey	OSB
Reading	OSB
Buildwas	OCist
Waltham	OSA
Crowland	OSB
Melrose	OCist
Cirencester	OSA
Kelso	OSB
Combe	OCist
St Andrews	OSA
Eynsham	OSB
Much Wenlock	Cluniac

REGISTRUM C. 1290	MLGB TO 1540	BIG CAT. (*various dates*)	AGGREGATE	IS *REGISTRUM* THE MAIN EVIDENCE?
362	153	—	250	*yes*
356	361	1,831	—	
248	4	—	—	*yes*
246	271	261	2,000	
242	4	—	—	*yes*
240	3	—	9	*yes*
231	29	—	—	*yes*
184	12	—	4	*yes*
168	151	297	585	
160	7	—	—	*yes*
159	2	—	—	*yes*
153	5	—	—	*yes*
146	217	—	—	
135	29	160	300	
128	27	—	20	*yes*
123	34	653	750	
114	131	204	250	
112	54	—	—	
111	27	132	—	
110	19	96	—	*yes*
102	1	—	—	*yes*
98	40	—	10	
96	1	—	—	*yes*
95	1	—	—	*yes*
95	8	—	—	*yes*
92	8	—	12	*yes*
92	6	—	—	*yes*

their return to the headquarters of the project at the Oxford Grey Friars.[46] For a fair number of these institutions, *Registrum* provides more evidence, in some cases much more evidence, than any other source, for example institutions in Scotland such as Kelso or Melrose, whose returns give the impression of a substantial library that we would otherwise not know about. But it is impossible to form much picture of a collection from the entries in *Registrum*.

The library of Woburn (Beds.), for example, is attested in the 1290s by 248 titles entered in *Registrum Anglie*, but other evidence for the medieval library is a single manuscript of the twelfth century, which had left Woburn in time to be acquired by William Gray and given to Balliol College, Oxford, in the fifteenth century. Besides this, *MLGB*3 knows three printed books, two acquired by the abbot in the 1520s, one by a monk in 1537, a year before the remaining monks of the abbey were attainted and executed. Without *Registrum* the Cistercian library at Woburn would be a void filled only by assumption. For close to two-thirds of the institutions in this upper range of entries in *Registrum*, the evidence of *Registrum* is fuller than can be got from *MLGB* or from any local documentation.

To fulfil the promise made in Chapter 1, to the effect that medieval library catalogues show us libraries as they once were, we must focus on true catalogues, allowing that inventories can add a sense of the size of collections and of their subject emphasis (an inventory heavy in canon law will be obvious even with little detail in the record) but they rarely add richness to the picture. I mentioned earlier that there are only about fifty true catalogues, some of them quite basic in their information, some of them very rich indeed. Reading these catalogues, as presented in the Corpus, is the best way to get to know medieval libraries as distinct from medieval books. The notes on the catalogues will always mention if and where the individual books are known to survive, as listed in *MLGB*, and the editor of the catalogue will have drawn as much information as possible from the actual books to enrich the interpretation offered alongside the catalogue itself.

Now, the old approach was to favour the biggest and best. M.R. James edited the catalogues from Christ Church Canterbury, from St Augustine's Canterbury, from Dover, from Peterborough, from Leicester, while Mary Bateson edited the Syon Abbey catalogue, but we risk misleading ourselves if we think libraries of more than a thousand volumes were in any sense typical.[47] These catalogues are all in their different ways exceptional, and the St Augustine's catalogue is in some ways the most remarkable and challenging. It was presented by M.R. James as a catalogue of the late fifteenth century. It seeks to structure itself as an aid to finding copies of particular works, batching by author and work, and also introducing cross-references to copies bound in other books. But it was worked on and augmented for a century or so, and it took the extraordinary work of Bruce Barker-Benfield to work out that this was a catalogue of the late fourteenth century, much augmented and then recopied in the late fifteenth century, so that layers of additions had been flattened out in the recopying.[48] To truly understand and interrogate a catalogue of this scale is a massive task. Around the time the cataloguer was working at St Augustine's, Henry de Kirkestede was working at Bury, and John Whitfield at Dover, all within the space of twenty or thirty years. The 1360s to the 1380s was the period when cataloguing and metadata were at their most flourishing, more than at any other period in the Middle Ages.

The enthusiast for medieval libraries will no doubt read all fifty catalogues and benefit proportionately. One can form an overall picture that way, but there is a risk that different lists will cross-fertilize, or should I say cross-infect. If we want to be able to characterize libraries, we need a typology of catalogues to reflect the different types of library in England. My assumption – or, to use a less prejudicial word, my hypothesis – is that our typology will most likely have to reflect

TABLE 9 Twelfth-century catalogues in date order

PLACE	SPECIES	REF.	DESCRIPTION	DATE	NO.
Peterborough	OSB	BP2	List of titles in the library, early 12th cent.	1120	59
Rochester	OSB	B77	Catalogue of the library, 1123	1123	100
Durham	OSB	BD5	Catalogue of the library, mid-12th cent.	1160	456
Lincoln	cath	SC59	Catalogue, *c.* 1170	1170	105
Burton-on-Trent	OSB	B11	List of books in the library, *c.* 1175	1175	70
Bury St Edmunds	OSB	B13	Catalogue of the library, late 12th cent, with additions	1175	261
Rievaulx	OCist	Z19	First catalogue, late 12th cent.	1190	225
Welbeck	OPrem	P9	Catalogue, late 12th cent.	1190	113
Whitby	OSB	B109	Catalogue of the library, late 12th cent.	1190	86
Reading	OSB	B71	Catalogue of the library, *c.* 1192	1192	204
Reading Leominster	OSB	B75	List of books kept at the cell of Leominster, *c.* 1192	1192	77
Bridlington	OSA	A4	List of books in *Armarium Magnum*, late 12th/early 13th cent.	1200	118
Rievaulx	OCist	Z20	Second catalogue, late 12th cent.	1200	208
Waltham	OSA	A38	Catalogue of books, late 12th/early 13th cent.	1200	132

TABLE 10 Twelfth-century catalogues in size order

PLACE	SPECIES	REF.	DESCRIPTION	DATE	NO.
Durham	OSB	BD05	Catalogue of the library, mid-12th cent.	1160	456
Bury St Edmunds	OSB	B013	Catalogue of the library, late 12th cent., with additions	1175	261
Rievaulx	OCist	Z19	First catalogue, late 12th cent.	1190	225
Rievaulx	OCist	Z20	Second catalogue, late 12th cent.	1200	208
Reading	OSB	B071	Catalogue of the library, *c.* 1192	1192	204
Waltham	OSA	A38	Catalogue of books, late 12th/early 13th cent.	1200	132
Bridlington	OSA	A04	List of books in *Armarium Magnum*, late 12th/early 13th cent.	1200	118
Welbeck	OPrem	P9	Catalogue, late 12th cent.	1190	113
Lincoln	cath	SC59	Catalogue, *c.* 1170	1170	105
Rochester	OSB	B077	Catalogue of the library, 1123	1123	100
Whitby	OSB	B109	Catalogue of the library, late 12th cent.	1190	86
Reading Leominster	OSB	B075	List of books kept at the cell of Leominster, *c.* 1192	1192	77
Burton-on-Trent	OSB	B011	List of books in the library, *c.* 1175	1175	70
Peterborough	OSB	BP02	List of titles in the library, early 12th cent.	1120	59

three dimensions of difference. Let us suppose, until we have evidence to convince us otherwise, that Benedictine, Cistercian, Carthusian, Augustinian libraries may have differed from one another in some fundamental ways, that the libraries of the mendicant orders very likely differed more, and that the libraries of secular institutions, whether cathedrals or collegiate churches or university colleges, all had different needs and interests. Not all Benedictine libraries were the same, however, and a crucial factor is one of scale. Take Dover and Deeping, both priories dependent on Benedictine abbeys: Dover (Kent), a cell of Canterbury, had 450 books in 1389, catalogued by Whitfield as if they were expected to stay in Dover and were not on deposit from the library of the mother house, while Deeping (Lincs.), a cell of the prosperous Fenland abbey of Thorney (Cambs.), had 22 books in the monks' aumbry in the mid-fourteenth century, and they do seem to be books deposited there from Thorney. It is not unusual for cells to take and return books from the mother house, so Dover is the one that appears exceptional here, a cell with a (relatively) large library that was not typical. Divergences of scale, not necessarily related to the wealth of the house or the number of its monks, canons or friars, apply to all the other kinds of institution too. These places may have had large, middling or small libraries, and we need to seek out catalogues that will provide us with a type for a middling or a small example as well as for the greatest collections in the land. If we do not have a scheme of types for this purpose, we cannot rightly picture the plausible context for reading or writing but generalize too blandly. And if we generalize from the best known big catalogues, we falsify.

After order and scale, the third dimension of difference is chronological. All institutions change over hundreds of years and the same is absolutely the case with libraries. We may make the supposition that libraries start small and get bigger, so small at a late date tells us more about scale than small at an early date. What we cannot well demonstrate is the phenomenon of reshaping collections to meet current needs, a polite way of referring to deaccessioning. In some libraries at the present this is a pervasive concern, and the modernization of libraries in the late fifteenth and sixteenth centuries by the accession of large numbers of printed books shows that it was not absent from the Middle Ages.

In one sense our difficulty is insufficient evidence of the quality we should wish for, but wishing for better is a matter for fantasy, not reality. Our real difficulty is in choosing the most reliable types according to our three dimensions among the evidence that we have. All the catalogues from the twelfth century are grouped in TABLES 9 & 10. The earliest is from Peterborough, 59 entries, quite modest by comparison with numbers already discussed. In the late fourteenth century another Peterborough catalogue (BP21) had 348 entries, not impressive alongside Canterbury or Bury, but not insignificant. We can hypothesize therefore that Peterborough represents a middling Benedictine library, one that grew substantially over the twelfth to fourteenth centuries, and we shall find that growth discussed in the introduction to the volume in the Corpus dedicated to Peterborough abbey. It and Dover are the two middling Benedictine libraries that have their own volumes in the Corpus. Now, Peterborough was much bigger and richer than Dover, and if the monks had wanted it one must suppose that they could have had a much bigger and better library. Dover, on the other hand, was batting above its rank. On the same two tables Durham shows very impressively. We know that by the end of the fourteenth century Durham was not really in competition with big libraries such as Bury and Canterbury, but in the twelfth century it looks as if it had got off the mark quicker.[49] In my judgement Durham was always one of the larger libraries and its catalogues should be read with that in mind.

From the thirteenth century this sort of evidence is very thin on the ground. The extant catalogues in sequences of both date and size

TABLE 11 Thirteenth-century catalogues in date order

PLACE	SPECIES	REF.	DESCRIPTION	DATE	NO.
Rochester	OSB	B79	Catalogue of the library, 1202	1202	241
Flaxley	OCist	Z7	Catalogue, early 13th cent.	1210	80
Glastonbury	OSB	B39	Catalogue of the library, 1247/8, with additions	1248	402
Carisbrooke (Lyre)	OSB	B17	List of books at Stuleg and Carisbrooke, 1260, with additions	1260	18
Bradsole	OPrem	P2	Catalogue, late 13th cent.	1290	147

are represented in TABLES 11 & 12. Glastonbury, one of the oldest and richest abbeys in England, had in the mid-thirteenth century a library comparable in size – but not, I think, in quality – with that of Durham a century earlier. It seems to have been a middling type for the period, but there is no good quality type at all in the thirteenth century. We can, none the less, avoid the thought that there had been a major setback in Benedictine libraries since the twelfth century. If the twelfth-century books had been lost in a period of decline, they could not survive today, and places like Bury and Durham, Reading and Rochester, are well represented still by twelfth-century books. Glastonbury, therefore, despite its size and opulence, was underinvested in its library at this date. Whether it picked up or declined later we have scarcely the means to guess.

From the fourteenth century we see the largest number of catalogues, and the largest number of entries in catalogues (TABLES 13 & 14). If the inventories from university colleges were to be added, we should also see more middling collections and perhaps even some

TABLE 12 Thirteenth-century catalogues in size order

PLACE	SPECIES	REF.	DESCRIPTION	DATE	NO.
Glastonbury	OSB	B39	Catalogue of the library, 1247/8, with additions	1248	402
Rochester	OSB	B79	Catalogue of the library, 1202	1202	241
Bradsole	OPrem	P2	Catalogue, late 13th cent.	1290	147
Flaxley	OCist	Z7	Catalogue, early 13th cent.	1210	80
Carisbrooke (Lyre)	OSB	B17	List of books at Stuleg and Carisbrooke, 1260, with additions	1260	18

large ones. The fifteenth century (TABLES 15 & 16) is represented by a decline in catalogues and an increase in inventories, very possibly corresponding to a shift in the weight of evidence away from religious institutions, which no longer kept up with the universities in their book provision. In this respect a factor we have not attempted to include is the simple number of personnel to be provided for. Colleges existed primarily to support godly learning. They had far fewer fellows than the complement of monks in a major religious house, but here too we should need to confront change that is not easily documented. The number of monks in many religious houses was not by any means constant, and we do not have the means to know the peaks and troughs. A house that was managing its books to meet its current needs might have had occasion to shrink its library quite drastically, but new interests in books and in the texts to be read might provoke expansion. In the fifteenth century the type site must be Syon with its large library, modern in every sense, a foundation of the early fifteenth century, with a modern devotional interest and quickly moving into

TABLE 13 Fourteenth-century catalogues in date order

PLACE	SPECIES	REF.	DESCRIPTION	DATE	NO.
Bermondsey	Cluniac	B10	Catalogue of a library, perhaps Bermondsey, 1310 × 1328	1320	114
Canterbury Christ Church	OSB	BC5	Catalogue of the library, 1326	1326	1,831
London Dominicans	OP	F31	Catalogue of the library by Richard de Winkele, 1339, as excerpted by Bale	1339	13
Ramsey	OSB	B67	Fragment of a catalogue of books, mid-14th cent.	1340	198
Durham	OSB	BD10	Fragment of a catalogue of the Spendement, *c.* 1345	1345	140
Ramsey	OSB	B68	Fragment of a catalogue of books, mid-14th cent.	1350	609
Thorney Deeping	OSB	B102	List of books in the monks' *armariolum*, 14th cent.	1350	22
Llanthony	OSA	A16	Catalogue of the library, *c.* 1355–60	1360	508
Hulne Carmelites	OCarm	F16	Catalogue, 1366	1366	87
York Austins	OESA	F56	Catalogue of the library, 1372, with additions	1372	646
Canterbury St Augustine's	OSB	BA1	Catalogue of the library, late 14th cent., continued to late 15th cent.	1380	1,837
Aylesford	OCarm	F1	Part of catalogue, 1381	1381	14
Dover	OSB	BM1	John Whitfield's catalogue of the library, 1389	1389	450
Peterborough	OSB	BP21	Catalogue, late 14th cent.	1390	348
Durham	OSB	BD11	Catalogue of books in the Spendement, 1392 onwards	1392	516
Durham	OSB	BD12	Catalogue of books in the Cloister, 1395	1395	386
Meaux	OCist	Z14	Catalogue of books, 1396	1396	363
Titchfield	OPrem	P6	Catalogue of the library, Michaelmas 1400	1400	241

TABLE 14 Fourteenth-century catalogues in size order

PLACE	SPECIES	REF.	DESCRIPTION	DATE	NO.
Canterbury St Augustine's	OSB	BA1	Catalogue of the library, late 14th cent., continued to late 15th cent.	1380	1,837
Canterbury Christ Church	OSB	BC5	Catalogue of the library, 1326	1326	1,831
Ramsey	OSB	B68	Fragment of a catalogue of books, mid-14th cent.	1350	609
Ramsey	OSB	B67	Fragment of a catalogue of books, mid-14th cent.	1340	198
Durham	OSB	BD11	Catalogue of books in the Spendement, 1392 onwards	1392	516
Durham	OSB	BD12	Catalogue of books in the Cloister, 1395	1395	386
York Austins	OESA	F56	Catalogue of the library, 1372	1372	
York Austins	OESA	F56	Catalogue of the library, 1372, with additions, 1392	1392	646
Llanthony	OSA	A16	Catalogue of the library, *c.* 1355–60	1360	508
Dover	OSB	BM1	John Whitfield's catalogue of the library, 1389	1389	450
Meaux	OCist	Z14	Catalogue of books, 1396	1396	363
Peterborough	OSB	BP21	Catalogue, late 14th cent.	1390	348
Titchfield	OPrem	P6	Catalogue of the library, Michaelmas 1400	1400	241
Bermondsey	Cluniac	B10	Catalogue of a library, perhaps Bermondsey, 1310 × 1328	1320	114
Hulne Carmelites	OCarm	F16	Catalogue, 1366	1366	87
Thorney Deeping	OSB	B102	List of books in the monks' *armariolum*, 14th cent.	1350	22
Aylesford	OCarm	F1	Part of catalogue, 1381	1381	14
London Dominicans	OP	F31	Catalogue of the library by Richard de Winkele, 1339, as excerpted by Bale	1339	13

TABLE 15 Fifteenth-century catalogues in date order

PLACE	SPECIES	REF.	DESCRIPTION	DATE	NO.
Lincoln	cath	SC64	Booklist, *c.* 1411	1411	32
Cambridge Peterhouse	coll	UC48	Catalogue, 24 December 1418	1418	456
Hulne Carmelites	OCarm	F17	Catalogue, 1433	1433	45
York St Mary's	OSB	B120	Index catalogue of selected authors, 15th cent.	1440	653
Thurgarton	OSA	A36	Fragment of a catalogue of books and booklets, 15th cent.	1450	47
Lincoln	cath	SC68	Catalogue of chained books, after 1454	1455	109
London Guildhall	town	SH47	List of books, *c.* 1470	1470	14
Darlington	coll	SC222	List of books in the library, 1487	1487	16
Leicester	OSA	A20	Catalogue of books, 1463, 1477 × 1494	1490	941
Syon	OSS	SS1	Catalogue of the library by Thomas Betson, *c.* 1500, with additions, *c.* 1524	1524	1,464

TABLE 16 Fifteenth-century catalogues in size order

PLACE	SPECIES	REF.	DESCRIPTION	DATE	NO.
Syon	OSS	SS1	Catalogue of the library by Thomas Betson, *c.* 1500, with additions, *c.* 1524	1524	1,464
Leicester	OSA	A20	Catalogue of books, 1463, 1477 × 1494	1490	941
York St Mary's	OSB	B120	Index catalogue of selected authors, 15th cent.	1440	653
Cambridge Peterhouse	coll	UC48	Catalogue, 24 December 1418	1418	456
Lincoln	cath	SC68	Catalogue of chained books, after 1454	1455	109
Thurgarton	OSA	A36	Fragment of a catalogue of books and booklets, 15th cent.	1450	47
Hulne Carmelites	OCarm	F17	Catalogue, 1433	1433	45
Lincoln	cath	SC64	Booklist, *c.* 1411	1411	32
Darlington	coll	SC222	List of books in the library, 1487	1487	16
London Guildhall	town	SH47	List of books, *c.* 1470	1470	14

printed books in the later part of the century. Our difficulty lies in guessing whether it was on its own or whether other houses were moving in the same direction.

Now, I feel as if I ought to have arrived at a conclusion that should allow me to say, roughly, in a range of numbers, how many entries a catalogue should have that will serve as a type for a small, middling or large library, of this or that species, in each of these four centuries, but I am not confident that I can reduce it to such convenient simplicity, and I am appalled by the gaps. When all the evidence for the libraries of the mendicant orders is assembled, we see no sign of a backdrop against which the York Austin friars' library of more than 600 volumes in the late fourteenth century will seem ordinary. The rest of the evidence for the mendicants is desperately poor and I am sure that is in large part for lack of evidence. We simply cannot see the major libraries that at least the Grey Friars and Black Friars formed at Oxford and Cambridge in the thirteenth century, libraries that were the backdrop of much scholarship that in turn expanded and influenced life in the universities. At a later date, the friaries of London look as though they should have been major libraries, but the evidence has gone so we cannot fill all the slots in attempting to frame a typology. Yet the typological approach still seems the right one to adopt to catalogues, in the hope of gaining an overview of library distribution around the country, even though the evidence leaves us struggling. That is, none the less, better than to generalize from the richest evidence and so paint a false picture.

MLGB and the Corpus of British Medieval Library Catalogues are complex bodies of data that can be used simply. Do we know where this book once was? Were there copies of (say) Bede's biblical commentaries in a particular place? Were they widely known in England in the later Middle Ages? These are specifics. But these complementary bodies of evidence may also be interrogated as witnesses more generally to the diverse and developing landscape of medieval libraries.

THREE

Library Books and Personal Books

IF WE ARE ACCUSTOMED to using in a simple way two complex bodies of evidence for medieval libraries – books that carry marks of institutional provenance, and library catalogues that seek to portray a whole collection of books at a particular time – this evidence also has the potential to answer bigger, more general, questions. Without losing sight of libraries as institutional holders of book collections, the purpose of this chapter is to examine how the same bodies of evidence can offer reflections of books owned by individuals.

It is in the nature of a database to atomize information and hamper good visual communication, something we tried to avoid in *MLGB*3, which retains much of the former layout on the printed page. The chance to open up details behind the single-line entry means that information from the original record card can be made available, something that was very difficult for Ker to achieve in the printed book. He sacrificed the wording of *ex libris* inscriptions, for example, on the grounds that they are generic; an *ex libris* is a simple signification of institutional ownership. But their pattern over time in a particular house can be crucial for conveying how well managed the library was. He did include the wording of inscriptions referring to donors or those that provide other non-generic evidence of provenance, and this list of donor-dominated inscriptions occupies one hundred pages, organized at first level by institution and at second level by alphabetical order of name, which is inconvenient when turning from the library entry to the donors' list with only a shelfmark to go on. These hundred pages represent a considerable body of evidence for personal ownership of what are by definition library books. I am not conscious that it has ever been used as a resource. In *MLGB3* the data is invisible on the virtual cards behind each line, convenient for getting behind the evidence for a specific book, difficult for general appraisal, for example over time or by the distribution of donors between one kind of institution and another.

Library catalogues can provide the same kind of information, naming the donors of individual books or even listing books under a heading for a particular donor who gave multiple books. We shall also see that among our thousand-plus library records, a large class comprises not catalogues but records of accession, in most cases by gift from a named donor, and another large class comprises records of intention to give, not necessarily fulfilled. A list in a monastic context of books given by an abbot we take to represent accession. Sometimes bequests are recorded in the same way as, in effect, a record of receipt. A will that leaves books to a particular institution, or institutions, is evidence of books in private hands and potential evidence that the books went to their intended beneficiary. This can sometimes be proven by matching a document to a book bearing an inscription with the name, but, with only a will to show, one did not know whether the books were delivered or, supposing they were, whether they were accessioned rather than sold on.

The Corpus has included some 560 accession records, of which wills represent the great majority. The number of entries as itemized from this class of record is around 6,600. As a proportion of documents, this is by far the most numerous species of record; but as a proportion of entries, which roughly equates with books, 6,600 is quite small in relation to the 50,000 entries represented by all the documents. None the less, between *MLGB* and the Corpus there is considerable data about books that passed from personal ownership into institutional ownership.

It is important to keep in mind the reality of personal books. Two copies of the Life of St Modwenna, by Geoffrey, abbot of Burton-on-Trent, make a helpful illustration.[50] BL MS. Royal 15 B. IV (s. xii/xiii) is obviously a private book. The layout of the page, almost square and quite small, 180 by 165 mm, the lack of margin, the small handwriting when there is no particular need for such economy, the lack of ruling, are all signs that say this was an unprofessional copy made by someone who simply wanted to own the work. The book in which it is now bound comprises twenty-five textual items, not all of them complete, in twenty-six gatherings. They range from grammar to Euclid to excerpts from papal letters going beyond what found its way into decretal collections. The handwriting spreads across probably more than a generation. When they were first bound together is impossible to say, but at the end of the Middle Ages they were certainly a single book with a label on the back cover recognizable as that of Worcester cathedral priory. The volume has a Worcester pressmark, 'aa.xi'.

A reasonable guess would be that these booklets, which may well have more than one personal origin, were bound together, most likely at Worcester and most likely in the thirteenth century, and simply stayed there. The volume was still at Worcester when Humfrey Wanley compiled the cathedral's entry for *Catalogi manuscriptorum Angliae et Hiberniae* in the 1690s. By 1734 it was in the old Royal collection. So, reading the signs, this was a personal book that became an institutional book. The maker may have been a monk, but the opportunity to copy the Life of St Modwenna is unexplained. We must eschew the lazy assumption that it was made at, still less for, Burton abbey.

The second example is another, rather better and more complete copy of the Life and Miracles of St Modwenna, BL MS. Add. 57533.

This is perhaps a little older than the personal copy and it obviously exhibits more (to use Malcolm Parkes's word) decorum in script and layout. That argues for professional production, but it does not make it a library book. The date of writing is not earlier than January 1198, for the book contains a copy of *De miseria conditionis humanae*, and in the rubric to this the author is referred to as Pope Innocent III, and he was elected 8 January. It is not very much later. This copy of the Pope's work is one of a dozen still surviving made in different places in England that the palaeographical eye would date to s. xii/xiii or s. xiii^{in}. What they represent is the circulation of the new pope's book, composed by Cardinal Lotharius in the winter of 1194–5 to prove that he was not just a clever lawyer but could teach spirituality. He had published the book early in 1195 to improve his chances of election when the old Celestine III died, and he gave out copies as booklets to cardinals or other influential figures. His election as pope provoked international demand, and one or more booklets circulated in England from religious house to religious house. At some, perhaps at many, a copy was made to keep, and the booklet was passed on.

The contents of this volume are an odd mixture: Aelred of Rievaulx's Life of St Edward the Confessor and his earlier Life of King David of Scotland, which shows David's and Henry II's descent from the West Saxon kings; the *Miracles of the Virgin* (as found also in Balliol College, MS. 240), with two sermons on the Virgin by Fulbert of Chartres, which must have travelled with the text; Innocent III's *De miseria*; each continuing in the same quire as the previous text. And then Geoffrey of Burton's Life of St Modwenna, written, I think, by the same hand but starting in a new quire. The Life is completed in four quires, three regular ones and the fourth with one added leaf. The Life was therefore a self-standing unit within the manuscript, but, apart from some difference in the initials, looking exactly like it was meant to be there. Knowing what we do about the *De miseria*, I conjecture that, wherever this was written, there was a scribe at work with a book of diverse texts in progress unbound on his writing desk. When the Pope's book arrived, a decision was taken to copy it, and the decision to copy the Life of St Modwenna may represent similar opportunism, though the text was in this case fifty years old. It is not a widely known work.[51] Ker entered this volume under Burton in *MLGB2* at galley-proof stage after finding it mentioned under Balliol MS. 240 in Mynors' catalogue, then newly published, but it appears now as rejected: the mere fact of including Modwenna's Life had been enough for the then owner, Francis Wormald, to tell Mynors that his book was from Burton, but for obvious reasons Ker did not accept that as evidence of provenance.

More than twenty years ago, I was reading the draft of Tessa Webber's edition of the late-fifteenth-century Leicester abbey catalogue in my capacity as general editor of the Corpus, when I recognized the itemization of mixed contents of this volume (A20. 660):

> Vita sancti regis Edwardi in asseribus cum albo coopertorio
> 2° fo. *cior quo nemo*
> Vita sancti Dauid regis Scocie
> Miracula sancte Marie
> Vita sancte Modwenne

The catalogue gives the second folio, *cior quo nemo sullimior* (in context *nemo sanc|tior, quo nemo sublimior*; *PL* 195. 740D), and at once I phoned Michelle Brown in the British Library to ask her to check the second folio in the actual manuscript. She did, and it was a hit, so this book could be provenanced to Leicester abbey around 1490. Whether it had been there all its working life we cannot say, but I think the likely context of its making means it was created as a library book. Soon after its entry in the Leicester catalogue, the book left the library, acquiring an inscription by Hector Riding, the vicar of Ratcliffe on Soar (Notts.) between 1497 and 1509, and it remained in private collections until 1971.

We have observed the differences between a personally made book and a professionally made book, both of them plausibly made within a monastic or canonical context. One might ask if there is any difference between a privately owned book and one institutionally owned, but the answer to that is difficult to perceive. Books without clear evidence of institutional provenance may none the less have been in libraries.

When we think about production, however, there is a long tradition of fusing institutional ownership and institutional production, the notion of the monastic *scriptorium*. This idea persists in two senses: it has existed in the minds of antiquaries for three or four hundred years, and the scriptorium itself is seen as having endured as a means of in-house production from the seventh century or earlier to the late Middle Ages. By contrast, modern work on manuscript production in later medieval England is focused on professional, often called commercial, production between the late fourteenth century and whenever the demand for manuscript books faded out in the face of the spread of cheaper printed books in the late fifteenth century. Between those two phases, a phase in which we pay attention to monastic scriptoria and a phase when we believe firmly in commercial production, there is a longish period of around two hundred years that receives a good deal less attention. I should argue that commercial production can be taken back into the mid-thirteenth century and very plausibly earlier.

The evidence from library records shows a similar phasing. Down to *c.* 1160 two major catalogues show foundation collections that can be equated with monastic scriptoria; but after that date down to the time of the catalogues themselves, in the second quarter of the fourteenth century, accessions are represented by donors, listing books under headings for this or that name. Two such are the catalogue from Christ Church Canterbury drawn up around 1326 in the time of Prior Henry of Eastry (BC5) and the slightly later catalogue from Ramsey abbey, not before 1328 (B67–68).[52] After the mid-fourteenth century we do not have catalogues organized in this way, inventories are less likely to record donors' names, and the shape of the evidence shifts. Now, between the 1320s and the third quarter of the century, which saw a new sophistication in catalogues, it is possible that Benedictine libraries, at least, were woken up from intellectual quietude by the bull *Summi magistri*, which required the richer monasteries to send a monk or two to study at the universities, and books and libraries began to matter more.[53] The fact of accessions simply through the accident of donation by members of the community suggests no great interest in collection development. It leads to multiple copies of basic texts in a library.

Against this background, two modes of collection development merit attention. The first is centred on the twelfth century down to *c.*1160 and dominated by the idea of planned library expansion by means of a monastic scriptorium. The second, dominant in Benedictine evidence from *c.*1160 to the mid-fourteenth century, is defined by accession that arrived mostly through 'gifts', usually the transfer of personal books held by individual monks to their abbey in line with the principle that monks had no private property. We encountered a late and large example in the first chapter, when more than two hundred books belonging to Cardinal Adam Easton were shipped back to England and accessioned at the house of his first profession, Norwich cathedral priory.

During much of the fourteenth and fifteenth centuries, the library records, as we have seen, show a pattern of increasing preponderance of secular information in the record, accompanied by the large change in the proportion of secular-owned books in *MLGB3* resulting from the inclusion of books from and in university colleges. The university setting is one in which personal or quasi-personal books come to dominate within college collections, often built up by gifts from previous members or patrons of the college, often given on long loan to individuals. College collections are in a close relationship with personal books. The books from the monastic colleges are far less visible to us, and there is a suspicion that the university provided an environment for them to drift away from monastic ownership in the hands of students. We shall look at a very late monastic example from Syon Abbey, founded in 1417, where there is evidence of rapid growth in the library, but our dating of that growth relies on the record in the catalogue of the individual donors, who can in some cases be dated, albeit only quite broadly. Even a late-medieval foundation such as Syon built a library not by planned collection development but by apparently random donation.

What may persist in these various contexts is the underlying fact that different contexts had different needs, but in each case the needs of the individuals associated with the institution – whether Benedictine monks, secular clerks in the universities, or Bridgettine brethren at Syon – and of their institutions tended to align, so that unplanned accession did not lead to a great many unsuitable acquisitions.

Behind all this is the fundamental question, where do library books come from? Well-made books were made by scribes with professional skills, and a question one step further back is, where do professional scribes come from? To the first question there are five possible answers: domestic production by members of a community, hired scribes from outside, a bespoke order to professional producers outside the institution, plain purchase from outside the institution, and gift or bequest from within or without the community (though if from within then the question is pushed back one stage, how did the monk or canon acquire personal books?). When one considers production rather than ownership, a community had three areas of need for books: service books for the church, library books for study, and books kept and used in the management of the house and its estates. The means of production need not all be the same, but, by and large, professional quality was usual in all three areas.

Our thinking, especially with regard to the Anglo-Norman period, has been so dominated by monastic books and by the idea that they were produced in-house that we risk seeing a book economy in which libraries played the central role. The notion of the monastic scriptorium ought to be a more contentious one. Studies have focused on those libraries represented by good numbers of early- to mid-twelfth-century books in *MLGB* and treated them as evidence of integrated book production and learning. A key example would be the cathedral priory of Christ Church in Canterbury, where the distinctive spiky hand is a house script, associated only with the cathedral priory and with religious houses closely connected to it, St Augustine's abbey, Canterbury and Rochester cathedral priory. Ker in his Lyell Lectures taught us that exemplars for patristic texts came into Canterbury from Normandy and were shared around for copying in this period.[54] Tessa Webber has taught us that the spiky hand was very likely designed and passed on by Brother Eadmer, precentor of the cathedral, with responsibility for the books of both church and library.[55] Eadmer was also biographer of St Anselm, and Anselm's correspondence from time to time refers to getting something copied by certain brothers.[56] So we have a sense that Christ Church had a house script and could turn out books in-house or for neighbours, or share the exemplars with neighbours, where local monks did the writing.

Tessa Webber revealed the planned production of books to meet modern needs under the patronage of the bishops of Salisbury both earlier and later than the first practice of the spiky hand at Canterbury.[57] Bishop Osmund in the 1080s and 1090s had a group of scribes working for him, one of them being the scribe of Great Domesday, who needs also to be thought of in relation to the team of clerks who worked on that huge project. Francisco José Alvárez López's work on Exon Domesday, a manuscript now helpfully disbound in Exeter, shows a score of scribes working together, some much more engaged than others, on the extensive parchment work that lay behind the final synthesis of Great Domesday.[58] The number of clerks in the king's service, very likely in Salisbury to work on the six south-western counties, is no doubt surprising. Six to eight scribes working on books at Salisbury cathedral, in a secular environment, and then another group more than twenty years later, working for Bishop Roger, who from 1121 was the king's chief minister, tells a story of systematic collection development for the new cathedral that cannot be disputed.

At Salisbury the scribes were certainly secular, possibly members of the episcopal household, but possibly simply hired to work on a text over an extended period of time. Are we correct to extrapolate from Eadmer and Anselm that monks were the main labourers in the scriptorium? It is to be suspected that for a very long time scholars have been unconsciously led by depictions of writers in monastic environments, composing at writing lecterns: Lawrence of Durham, Vincent of Beauvais, and the famous Eadwine at the back of the Eadwine Psalter from Canterbury, now in Trinity College, Cambridge. But the tradition of depicting writers writing in copies of their books is not necessarily true to the environment of the scriptorium. While the iconography is always that of a writer composing, a true picture never encountered would depict a scribe copying with an exemplar open and the leaves of a new book in front of him.

The evidence for monk-scribes or canon-scribes is incontrovertible but sporadic. Among the accession lists in the Corpus which might be mentioned are the lists of books written by particular scribes. Brother Alexander at Rochester by 1203 had written nineteen books for the library, some of which are credited to him as donor in the catalogue of the library from 1202 (B80); the books in the list include library books and service books, and they do not overlap with the medical books added under the name of Alexander, sometime precentor, at the end of the 1202 catalogue (B79. 216–235). Brother John de Brugis at Coventry cathedral priory has left a list of thirty-three books written by him (B23): these are mostly church books but they include a book of charters and a few books for study, including what seems to be a copy of Gregory IX's *Decretales*, a big copying job. This was *c.* 1240. And not many years after that Brother William of Wycombe, a monk of Reading abbey, left a list of sixteen books, most of them liturgical, which he wrote at the behest of the precentor, the subprior, sometimes others, during a four-year stay at the cell of Leominster (B76); the books also include *excerpta*, for example, from the letters of Jerome and Augustine, so we have to suppose that Br. William was a reader as well as a copyist. His name is best known from a list of polyphony in BL MS. Harley 978, which includes the famous English song 'Sumer is icumen in'. One of his tasks was to add a copy of the pseudo-Augustinian *De spiritu et anima* to the copy of the Bible that Alfred of Dover bought, and we have a long account of this book, in the form of an open letter from Alfred, as sacrist of Reading, in which he gives a detailed description of this augmented Bible, which had been stolen from the cloister in 1253 (B73). Oxford, Bodleian Library, MS. Auct. F. 3. 8 is part of another book acquired by Alfred of Dover, with his name in it, so we have here a rather evocative cluster of monastic books connecting Reading and Leominster.

Much later, William Charite, who compiled the late-fifteenth-century catalogue from Leicester abbey (the one that John Nichols thought was a list of books with only two leaves), included books commissioned by him, books commissioned by him but in which he personally added the musical notation, books he wrote or compiled himself, and books he bought for the abbey (A20. 1878–1959). The total is 81 books, of which the largest component is 33 books bought, most of which can be found in their proper places in the catalogue. Only one of these (A20. 1055) can be matched with a survivor, now Edinburgh, National Library of Scotland, MS. Adv. 18.5.13, which was written in the late twelfth century and has a fifteenth-century inscription, *per acquisitionem fratris Willelmi Charyte*. This is one of a group of classical texts, schoolbooks no doubt, acquired by him that are listed together in the catalogue: one wonders whether the others which do not survive were also late-twelfth-century books, and one can only wonder where he was buying such books already three hundred years old.

However, occasional monk-scribes, or in William's case a canon-scribe, do not amount to planned collection development or a monastic scriptorium. For English historians, a classic account of the monastic scriptorium was provided by Sir Thomas Duffus Hardy in 1871, introducing the third volume of his impressive catalogue of the manuscript sources for medieval English history.[59] Here he provided several pages in rich detail about the management of the monastic scriptorium, as if describing some ideal, all of it taken from the twelfth-century *Liber ordinis* of the Paris abbey of Saint-Victor, which had been printed by Edmond Martène at the beginning of the eighteenth century.[60] Hardy did not so much as hint that there may have been something ideal about this, or that most religious houses did not see themselves as having a central role in making books available to the devout and learned of Europe as the abbey of Saint-Victor, near the centre of modern learning. Hardy was unaware that portions of this account of the well-regulated scriptorium were incorporated in the customs of Barnwell, near Cambridge, but their editor, John Willis Clark, certainly knew that they echoed the Saint-Victor *Liber ordinis* and imagined that all this was applicable, most improbably, in Barnwell.[61] Hardy had been reading the three volumes of the *Gesta abbatum* of St Albans, printed for the Rolls Series, of which he had oversight as Keeper of the Public Records, during 1867 to 1869, and here, in the text of the first volume, and in Riley's introduction in the third volume, he found valuable references to what is actually called the Scriptorium at St Albans. (The word commonly means a writing desk, and it is rare to find it used as an office where writing was carried out; *domus scriptorie*, the writing house, is a term more generally used for an office where business documents and accounts were written and kept. The *Medieval Latin Dictionary* offers no example of *scriptorius* as a neuter noun in the sense of *scriptorium*, having, surprisingly, missed the examples from the *Gesta abbatum*; it offers the word with only a couple of examples applied to the king's *scriptorium*, the staff of royal *scriptores*.)

From the *Gesta abbatum*, which for the twelfth century may have been written by contemporaries but was worked over by Matthew Paris in the thirteenth century and continued by Thomas Walsingham at the end of the fourteenth, Hardy found that Abbot Paul set up a scriptorium *c.* 1080 and brought in the best scribes from far away to write noble books for the abbey, which was embarked on its Norman rebuilding.[62] Twenty-eight unnamed books are referred to, with service books and precious *textus*, though it is unusual, and noteworthy, that the text mentions that exemplars were loaned to St Albans by Archbishop Lanfranc (Abbot Paul's uncle). This is not, presumably, meant to answer the problem of exemplars – how does one build a collection in-house, if one can only copy from what one already has? – but to show that the service books came from an authoritative source, the archbishop who was the promoter of new Benedictine customs in England. Under abbot after abbot mention is made of the writing of books, usually with specific reference to church books. By the middle of the twelfth century the scriptorium was stood down, because the abbey had enough books. But after 1166, Abbot Simon, a scholar, restarted the arrangement, keeping always two or three scribes in his chamber, and providing that future abbots should keep at least one. He revived the practice of earlier days that they should have daily rations from the cellar, so that their work should not be impeded by the need to go out and buy lunch.[63] (Had they been monks, their rations would have been automatic: and the reason why the rule of St Gilbert prohibited hired scribes from houses of the Gilbertine order was not to ensure that books were written by canons but to keep non-canons out of the house. Books could be bought in without the same risk as lay craftsmen.[64])

Whichever way one reads the evidence from St Albans, it does not point to a large airy room full of monks copying books. It shows hired scribes, evidently paid for, usually, by the abbot rather than by another officer with a dedicated funding stream. (Now, in the fourteenth century at St Albans we find a dispute between the sacrist and the *scriptorarius* about the maintenance of service books, and the abbot ruled that the sacrist should provide for the binding and repair of service books; the word *scriptorarius* is usually linked with the word *cantor*, as if synonymous, but the word is used only in the writings of Thomas Walsingham.[65]) The idea of hired scribes should present no difficulties. Wherever our manuscript with Innocent III's *De miseria* was written, one imagines a scribe retained on the payroll to write and copy as need demanded and opportunity allowed. That such a scribe might be directed by the precentor on behalf of abbot and chapter is entirely plausible, but it is equally plausible that an abbot may choose to direct their work himself. At Abingdon, under the Italian abbot Farizio at the beginning of the twelfth century, there was a campaign of library expansion, referred to in the history of the abbots simply in terms of many books in various subjects. But we are told specifically that Farizio hired six scribes for this work *preter claustrales*, in addition to those belonging to the house (B2). The monk-scribes were either not suitable for the work of library-building or were men already occupied in other writing work for the abbey, whether on service books or on business in the writing house.

The evidence that we have mostly shows that during a period of library expansion professional scribes were brought in from outside. Our sources do not mention where exemplars come from. Nor do they mention where scribes come from (beyond the reference in the *Gesta* to their coming from afar). One wonders whether hired scribes may actually have their own exemplars or access to them, and that by paying for the scribes one was also paying for the resources to which they had access. But the less challenging question remains: where in 1100 did Abbot Farizio go to hire six scribes? My answer – something I shall return to in what follows – is London. The idea that there was a period of collection development around the country between around 1080 or 1090 and around 1160 appears to be perfectly well founded.[66] The first phase was devoted to the renewal of collections with books that fitted a modern agenda for theology, the Bible, the emerging gloss and the Fathers, particularly the Latin Fathers. After 1140 or so, the second phases of this period of collection development included the acquisition of books of canon law and, towards the end of the period in question, books of civil law. But this was in a sense an externally imposed collection development: canon law was going through a period of serious renewal.[67] This was done by secular clerks in the service of the church, and its impact on monastic libraries was strictly secondary. Abbots and chapters were corporately affected by canon law, and naturally they liked to have the means to keep up. The study of civil law was not necessary for monastic life. In both areas of law we can and must assume that secular demand and secular production were making the running, and that monastic houses were for the most part buying into it.

On the margins, then, of the period when twentieth-century scholarship has tended to place libraries, and in particular monastic libraries, centre stage, there is clear and extensive evidence for a wider book economy outside. It is not isolated from or independent of the monastic environment. Geoffrey of Monmouth and Henry of Huntingdon were both archdeacons in the diocese of Lincoln in the time of Bishop Alexander. Ralph Gubiun, chaplain and keeper of the treasure to Bishop Alexander while still a secular priest, became a monk of St Albans but he continued to work on loan from the abbey to the bishop. He was a great lover of books, a persistent collector and an eager student of the Italian Master Guido, who lectured on the scriptures, seemingly in the bishop's household.[68] From 1146 Ralph became abbot of St Albans and he brought his secular books into the monastery.[69]

This pattern of books being added to monastic collections through individuals is visibly dominant, as mentioned above, in the catalogues of Christ Church Canterbury and Ramsey. It was empanelled in monastic custumals, which ordain that the name of the donor should be entered into each book, and that when a monk reads that book he should remember the donor in his prayers.[70] The assumption is that the donor, in most cases a monk, retained books for his personal use while he lived, and as monks had no private property they became part of the communal stock when he was in need of other readers' prayers. It is a pattern that can be recognized in the evidence from other Benedictine houses through the inclusion of donor names in the books rather than the organization of catalogues, but whether it applied in the stricter orders it is not possible to say. Augustinian houses do sometimes refer to donors but do not show the same organization that way, although the large catalogue from the late fifteenth century from Leicester ends with the addition of over thirty books from a specific donation (A20. 1926–1958).

From Ramsey abbey there are two imperfect copies of catalogues, one in codex form, of which only a few leaves have survived, now in Lambeth Palace Library, and a substantial roll, among the Cotton collection, which describe the same books under the same donors' names, though not always in the same words or in the same sequence (B67, B68). These fragments provide evidence of seventy-two donors, almost all of them monks, and among them Abbot Nicholas of

Reading (B67. 104–110, B68. 140–142), known from Reading sources as Nicholas of Whaplode, a village in the fens, where, a source from Lincoln tells us, his parents were buried.[71] No Reading source tells us that he was by profession a monk of Ramsey, later precentor and abbot of Reading, who retired to Ramsey in 1328 with his books. Some of these donors owned one or two books, often elementary. Some had remarkable personal collections. Both Robert of Dodford and Gregory of Huntingdon, in the mid-thirteenth century, owned books in Hebrew (B67. 51–68, 69–70, B68. 494–526, 527–543). Gregory also had books in Greek, of which one survives, a Greco-Latin psalter, now Cambridge, Corpus Christi College, MS. 468 (s. xiii). Walter of Lilford, an unknown figure, had an impressive collection of scholastic theology for the early fourteenth century (B68. 547–575), among them his own *reportationes* of the disputations he had attended, though neither of the two universities has preserved any record of his studying. Was he perhaps sent to Paris? He appears to have died as prior of the tiny cell of St Ives, from where his books came to the abbey.[72]

The evidence for libraries' acquiring books by gift is very extensive and contrasts with the slender basis for inferring any planned collection development over anything more than a short period. The very large number of accession records in the Corpus of British Medieval Library Catalogues has been mentioned above. Of those not simply classified as wills, the numbers tell a story. A simple bar chart might show that evidence of this kind grows steadily and steeply: from before 1100 CE we have 5 accession records, 1 by royal gift and 4 episcopal gifts of books to Benedictine houses. From the twelfth century the number of records is 7. From the thirteenth century it is 29, an increase that is not without interest, given that the number of actual known catalogues declines from the twelfth to the thirteenth century. Then from the fourteenth century we have 73 records of accession and from the fifteenth no fewer than 133. Even from the first part of the sixteenth century the tally is 65. Now, turning the figures round to look at them by the kind of institution recording receipt of books or accepting bequests, we find 69 Benedictine records, a striking number in the monastic context next to one Carthusian house, three Cistercian, three houses of Augustinian canons, and all of ten bequests to Franciscan friaries. There are none to Dominicans or to Austin friars. Now, it should be remembered that monks, canons and friars in ordinary circumstances did not make wills and were unable to bequeath property as private, so any testamentary gifts to these institutions came from outside. Many of the Benedictine records, however, are internal, recording the acquisition of books by members of the community, most often by abbots, paid for, one presumes, by the abbot's share of the communal revenues and becoming part of the common resources.

Accession records to secular cathedrals and to collegiate churches are more numerous, 43 for cathedrals, 34 for colleges, with 8 to hospitals and 8 to town or professional libraries. And to the university colleges, accession records from or in favour of university colleges number 128, and of the two universities 13. Among these 13 the three lists of books given to Oxford by Duke Humfrey itemize 274 books. Most accession records are not on that scale. Now, in addition to the 312 accession records broken down this way, there are some 240 further wills, all of them in favour of cathedrals, collegiate churches, hospitals or university colleges. A very small number of these documents attest to the bequest of a number of books approaching thirty, but the great majority show much smaller numbers: 6, 5, 4, and fewer.

Across the large number of documents it is difficult to control for whether there are references to books not going to institutions, and which therefore lie outside the scope of the Corpus. The general impression one gains is that there are not, but individual ownership of books is documented for individuals with very few books, often fewer than the monks whose books passed automatically into conventual stock. We have not yet worked out a sensible approach to the evidence for books in personal possession beyond those covered in this secondary way by the Corpus or by *MLGB* on the basis that they entered libraries and bear witness to that.

The upshot of all this is that books acquired and owned by individuals, whether monastic, secular or even lay, probably far outnumbered the holdings of libraries at every point during the period under review. The focus of scholarship on a palaeographical approach to twelfth-century books owned by a narrow range of institutions that have preserved them in numbers distorts the longer-term perceptions. It is obvious, not just from the hugely increased evidence of the later Middle Ages, that books for the most part were made in a secular book economy. Even for the twelfth century, if one reads historical sources from a monastic environment, or considers what some secular authors had been reading, the dimly attested book supply outside monastic libraries was probably greater than the better evidenced monastic collections. What the major collections did, and why we find them so interesting, is they preserved and accumulated in some cases many, many books. Catalogues and shelfmarks point to the large numbers, and a few libraries, as we saw, have left large numbers of monastic survivors. But it is also the case that some early libraries lost books, and the loss of monastic books fed the more mobile world of secular libraries. Turnover is the subject of the next chapter.

FOUR

Turnover in Libraries

THE PREVIOUS CHAPTER argued that the notion of the monastic scriptorium has coloured our general thinking too far; that, in the absence of very strong evidence, such as we have from Anglo-Norman Canterbury, it needs to be reinterpreted in terms of hired scribes, who may have been lay artisans; and that libraries and the production of books for libraries should be seen as part of a much larger book economy and not isolated from it. The role of donors has always been in evidence against the notion of planned collection development, and the fact that we know of gifts of books from the tenth and eleventh centuries, as well as our having a mass of evidence from the thirteenth to fifteenth centuries, invites us to think of secular book production as possible right across the period. The argument runs not against the notion that a campaign of copying might be organized for a short period of time but against the notion that those writing are assumed to be monks or canons.

The present chapter will seek to marshal evidence against another widespread assumption, namely that library books are assumed to continue in monastic and other libraries from their date of accession until the dissolution of religious houses between 1532 and 1540. Although books in private hands must find a new keeper and protector in every generation to survive, library books do have the chance of remaining unnoticed in the book cupboards of a large library for centuries. The example in Chapter 3 of a book formed by binding together twenty-five booklets, many of them personal copies of very diverse material, is a case in point, which may have lingered at Worcester for three centuries. This was probably never much used after the time of the owners of the booklets, but it was bound, and it got a pressmark around 1500. It would not have been missed, but there was very likely no second-hand market for it either.

That there was a second-hand market in books goes without saying. Parchment books were usually durable, and, in the absence of serious wear and tear, they could serve the needs of more than one generation. Owners and users of books often passed them on by bequest to successors with similar needs, and countless other books were sold and bought. We know all too little about this trade in the Middle Ages. In 1262 the sheriff of Oxford was ordered to produce one Reginald, stationer, of Oxford, to answer a claim in court from a clerk of the exchequer about a book worth 20 shillings, which was due to the clerk but held back by Reginald.[73] By the mid-fourteenth century *cautiones* are often found, books used as surety for loans of money, and a defaulter's book would be returned to the university stationers who had valued it, for sale at the amount of the loan plus a commission.[74] So, although the first catalogue of books printed for auction in England dates from 1676, the auctioning of books in Oxford is certainly attested before 1350. Such arrangements appear in Oxford statutes, but we have little sense of who was bidding for them, whether other students or dealers.[75]

It is a fact that libraries participated in the second-hand trade, but the circumstances are only dimly perceived. In the absence of direct evidence for deaccessioning, the easier approach is to look at libraries' buying of second-hand books. How readily available they were is not apparent. We have very little understanding of how a reader met his want for particular works, outside the very limited context of approved texts in the university setting.

I reprint here an important document, which was first excerpted by A.N.L. Munby in an article on the library of King's College, Cambridge. It was printed in full by James Willoughby in the headnote to Eton in his outstanding two-volume work on the libraries of the secular colleges, published in the Corpus.[76] It is a begging letter to King Henry VI from the provosts of his two foundations, Eton and King's, who found themselves in want of books, vestments and *ornamenta*, a word used for altar cloths and plate. The petition was submitted in March 1447, less than a month after the death of Oxford's great benefactor, Duke Humfrey, and it mentions access to the books and valuables of the late duke.

> Besechith mekely youre humble and trewe Orators the Provostes and Felowes of youre Two Colages Roiall of Eton' and Cambrigge, that for asmoche as thei ben' of youre Royall Fundacion nowe late fownded and newe growyng, and as yitte not so sufficyauntely stored in suche thinges as in verre trouthe of necessere and honeste moste nedes be had as Bokes for divine seruice and for theire lybraryes and theire studyes, Vestymentes, and other Onournements, whiche thinges may not be had with owte grete and diligente laboure be long processe and right besy inquisicion, please it to youre most noble grace to yeve in speciall commaundement and charge to maister Richard Chestre one of youre Chapellaynes that he take to hym suche men as shall be seen to hym expedient and profitable and in especiall John Pye youre Stacioner of London and other suche as ben connyng and haue vndirstonding in such matiers, charging hem and everich of hem to be assistant and helping hym with alle here diligence atte alle suche tymes as then shalle be required be the seid maister Richard for to laboure effectually in quere and diligently in serche in all place that ben vndir youre obeysaunse to gete knowleche where suche Bokes, Onourmentes and other necessaries for youre seid Colages may be founden to selle, grauntyng vnto the forsaid maister Richard youre full noble lettres patentz to be made in due fourme vndir youre grete Seall for to make

> suche Bokes and Ornementes where ever thei be founden to selle and make theym to be lawfully and resonably be praysed be men of gode conscience. And that doon it be lefull to hym to bye, take and receive alle suche goodes afore eny other man for the expedicion and profite of youre seid Colages, satisfying to the owners of suche godes suche pris as thei may resonably accorde and agree, soo that he may haue the ferste choise of alle suche goodes afore eny other man and in especiall of all maner <of> Bokes, ornementes and other necessaries as nowe late were perteynyng to the Duke of Gloucestre. And of youre habundaunt grace like it you to charge strettely the seid maister Richard that he doo alle his diligence and cesse not but alwey contynewe his laboure vnto suche tyme that youre seid Colages be sufficiently stuffid of suche bokes and necessaries as is afore rehersid. Taking the forseid maister Richard, his seruauntes, and theym that bene assistaunt and helpars to hym in this occupacioun vnto youre graciouse proteccion during the tyme of his laboure for youre seid Colages, and we shall euer pray god for you.

The request is for the right of privileged access to sellers, with a mechanism for agreeing a fair price, and it is implicit that the commodities wanted by the two colleges were hard to find. That may have been true or may in fact have been simply a pretext for asking for the king's help. One result was perhaps the gift to King's of what is now King's College, MS. 27, an English-made dedication copy of Antonio Beccaria's Latin translation of Athanasius' *Orationes*; Beccaria was Latin secretary to Duke Humfrey, and the book had certainly reached King's by 1453, when it was listed in the first library catalogue of the college (UC29. 80). Henry Bradshaw described it as 'the sole relic of the original library of the college', but it is a very exotic text. (A second volume is now BL MS. Royal 5 F. II.)

But what of Mr John Pye? He is to us a well-known London stationer with a long career, largely thanks to the work of Paul Christianson, whose *Directory of London Stationers and Book Artisans, 1300–1500* has gathered four pages of facts about him.[77] Among the data are half a dozen surviving books with inscriptions that indicate they were bought by individuals from John Pye. They were all new books at the time of purchase.

However, an examination of the early library of Eton College tells a different story. From 1465 we have an inventory of the valuables of the college, which includes an impressive array of choirbooks and 42 books in the library (SC229). The inventory gives only a few words about the text and the *secundo folio* of each book, but we are fortunate that eight of them remain in the college library. There is a late-thirteenth-century Galen, made in France, with no known earlier provenance (MS. 132; SC229. 121), and, rather more interestingly, a copy of Pierre de Tarentaise on the Pauline Epistles, written for St Albans abbey at the behest of Abbot Whethamstede before 1440, who paid 50 shillings for it (MS. 103; SC229. 103); it appears in a list of books given by him to the abbey and it has the abbey's *ex libris* and anathema. Yet, despite the anathema, it was given to Eton before 1465, almost certainly before 1461, while Whethamstede and Henry VI were both still alive and in office. But there are other monastic books here. There is a late-twelfth-century volume of notes on the Bible with thirteenth- and fourteenth-century *ex libris* inscriptions of Belvoir priory, a cell of St Albans, so possibly another gift, but more likely something bought in the second-hand market (MS. 48; SC229. 105). A three-volume collection of commentaries on the Old Testament, attributed in the booklist to Peter the Chanter, was written in England at the beginning of the thirteenth century and belonged to the Cistercians of Quarr abbey in the Isle of Wight (MSS 14, 16, 19; SC229. 97, 110, 96). When the Cistercians deaccessioned these volumes does not appear. Another surviving book cross-matched with an entry in the 1465 list has evidence of institutional ownership, sadly not yet interpreted: Eton College, MS. 15 (SC229. 94) has a fourteenth-century pressmark, '1ª partis 2ᵉ gradu, et in sinistro', not recognized. Now, if these survivors were already old books showing evidence of previously institutional ownership, then the buyer was buying among ex-library books and the 34 books in the list that do not survive may have been from a similar source.

Another library that was buying in the fifteenth century is that of the London Carmel. Thomas Netter, prior provincial in the 1410s and 1420s, invested money in increasing the library of the Carmelites in London, seemingly as a central resource for the order in England.[78] There is no booklist, alas, but the pressmarks of surviving books show that it was no small collection. Surviving books have marks in the form of letter and number, and taking the highest number in each letter class, A.1, C.24, F.18, I.79, M.57, and S.9, we can predict nearly two hundred books; if we allow ourselves to guess at fifty books at least under each letter from A to S, then we should predict nine hundred books in the collection. Seventeen books from the library survive, all but one bearing an early-fifteenth-century pressmark. Earliest is A.1, given by the leading Carmelite John Baconsthorpe in 1248 at the foundation of the London Carmel (now Oxford, Bodleian Library, MS. Laud Lat. 87). Several fourteenth-century books were received from members of the order, the usual pattern by which personal books were left to the house. Three were given as new books by Robert Ivory OCarm (d. 1392), prior provincial, and this slight evidence is given context by the lapsed Carmelite John Bale, who knew the London Carmel well in the early sixteenth century, and who tells us that Ivory 'wonderfully enlarged the library of his convent'.[79] There may have been many more books bought or commissioned by Ivory. But the present focus is on three books acquired by Thomas Netter in the early fifteenth century. Two of these were written in the twelfth century, the third datable to the turn of the twelfth and thirteenth centuries, so books more than two hundred years old when bought. One of them, now Oxford, Bodleian Library, MS. Bodl. 730, is a good monastic text, John Cassian's *Collationes*, and it has the *ex libris* of Buildwas abbey, a

Cistercian house in Shropshire, as well as that of the London Carmel and the Carmelite pressmark I.66.[80]

Now, a thirteenth-century glossed psalter from Buildwas came to Balliol College by gift of Robert Thwaites, who died in 1458. This is MS. 35A, which carries an inscription to show that it had been bequeathed to Buildwas abbey in 1277 by a secular master. No inscription reveals when it left Buildwas, which is 150 miles from London, and 100 miles from Oxford. Five further Buildwas books are now recognizable in Balliol. MS. 40 is inferred to be from there, since it was judged by Mynors to be 'from the same scriptorium' as MS. 150, which has the *ex libris* of Buildwas. MS. 173B has lost its *ex libris*, but it was at Balliol in the seventeenth century when copied by Gerard Langbaine. And MS. 229 also has the Buildwas *ex libris* and traces of an Oxford *cautio* from 1421: this was in Oxford to be annotated by Thomas Gascoigne (d. 1458), perhaps when it was already in the possession of his friend William Gray, who gave these five books to Balliol.[81]

Balliol was not buying books in the second-hand market, but its benefactors evidently were. Chief among the college library's benefactors was this William Gray, bishop of Ely. Among his gifts we find a Paris-made copy of Aquinas's *Quaestiones disputatae*, which was certainly the property of Ely cathedral priory in the first half of the fifteenth century; this no doubt found itself among Bishop Gray's books sometime after he was enthroned at Ely in 1459. It was not necessarily deaccessioned. Among the books given by Bishop Gray to Balliol there is a twelfth-century volume once owned by Lincoln cathedral, where Gray's uncle had been bishop and where he himself had held a canonry before 1431. There is a twelfth-century volume with the *ex libris* of Humberstone, a small Benedictine house in north Lincolnshire, from where no other book is known. There is a twelfth-century copy of Florus's compilation of Augustine on the Psalms from Woburn abbey (Beds.), the only manuscript known from that Cistercian house (though, as mentioned above, 248 titles from there appear in *Registrum Anglie*). There is a twelfth-century book from Bury St Edmunds, with its fourteenth-century *ex libris* and its fourteenth-century letter-mark, B.283, and Bury is a place not much associated by us with deaccessioning. Hardly less surprising is a copy of the sermons of Master Lawrence, who worked as a secular at Durham, became a monk at St Albans, and was elected abbot of Westminster: only one copy of his twelfth-century sermon compilation is known; it was seen at Westminster by Henry de Kirkestede in the fourteenth century (K358) and was at Balliol in the fifteenth (though with no known donor).[82] Again, Westminster is not normally judged to have been an institution inclined towards deacessioning books. There are two books from St Andrew's priory in Northampton, one of the twelfth century, the other of the thirteenth century, both given by Gray. Three other books from there are now in Oriel College: there is no evidence when or how they got there, but this adds to the sense that deaccessioning was happening at the priory. There is a thirteenth-century book from Chester abbey, which was still at Chester in the fourteenth century, and is now Balliol MS. 57, with an inscription from Chester in the hand that marked many books in the abbey; another of them, now Oxford, Bodleian Library, MS. Bodl. 373, would leave Chester and turn up in the fifteenth-century library of St George's Chapel at Windsor. Gray also gave a thirteenth-century book that had belonged to the Augustinian canons of Newark in Surrey (and three other books from there are now in Bodley, with no evidence of when or how they left Newark). There is a thirteenth-century book from St Osyth's priory in Essex and another from St Botolph's priory in Colchester, both small houses of Augustinian canons. There were two books belonging to the Franciscan convent in Cambridge, a late-thirteenth-century copy of Henry of Gent's *Quodlibeta* and an early fourteenth-century copy of St Bonaventure, which carries the name of a Franciscan from the mid-fifteenth century. Again, both were given by Bishop Gray. Another copy of Henry of Gent from the Cistercian abbey of Swineshead (Lincs.) came through Bishop Gray. No college in Oxford came to own so many ex-library books from religious houses during the middle years of the fifteenth century, and in Cambridge Peterhouse is the only rival, though not on such a large or diverse scale. (Of course, Peterhouse is one of the best documented of Cambridge libraries with a splendid and continuing fifteenth-century catalogue.)

How do books such as these come to leave their institutional homes and make their ways into the hands of Gray or other fifteenth-century collectors and benefactors of colleges? In one case at least there is an easy explanation: Balliol MS. 240 is from the small alien priory of Monks Kirby in Warwickshire, suppressed in 1415; it came to Balliol from Richard Bole, archdeacon of Ely, who was Gray's secretary and donor of a dozen books. If whatever books were at Monks Kirby came into the second-hand trade in 1415, Bole's picking up this copy did not happen until perhaps thirty years later. (Books from alien priories dissolved at this date are singularly rare.[83])

It appears from this tally that monastic houses of all sorts – except nunneries – were parting with books that were still desirable to a collector such as Gray. This is not the disposal of worn-out books or books whose contents appeared useless. If the books were worth Gray's while, they should have been worth keeping in their religious homes.

Perhaps the longest such tally of second-hand books is from St George's Chapel at Windsor Castle, founded by King Edward III in the middle of the fourteenth century. Its late medieval library is now best approached through the 82 surviving books, of which the great majority are preserved in the Bodleian Library by gift of the dean and canons in 1612. The chronology of these books' relationship with the Chapel is very difficult to establish. James Willoughby, in his treatment of the subject in his volumes for the Corpus on collegiate churches, printed extracts from the precentor's accounts and other dated records, among them a list of books, vestments, altar plate, and so on, from 1389, but it is difficult to match anything in this list with surviving books. A copy of Petrus Riga's *Aurora* may be the one that is now Oxford, Bodleian Library, MS. Bodl. 822, written in the early thirteenth century, which has no earlier provenance. No other from among the surviving books can be given a dated context in the documentary record. Willoughby, in his long headnote, draws the inference that 'a considerable expansion of the library must have taken place' after 1389.[84] In *MLGB1* Ker cautiously noted, 'It is not certain that all the books in the list belonged to Windsor before 1540', and in *MLGB2* he added, 'Many of them belonged to monastic houses before they came to Windsor; for details, see the index, pp. 374–80.' The indexed detail here is no more than the appearance of one or more provenances in addition to Windsor next to the modern shelfmarks (and I may say that in the index they are arranged alphabetically rather than sequentially, so that for places after Windsor in the alphabet the direction of travel appears to be from Windsor too, for example Worcester; further, no distinction is made between books with consecutive provenances and modern volumes that represent the binding together of items with independent provenances).[85] The *ex libris* inscriptions in surviving books from Windsor represent the charterhouse of Witham, Augustinian abbeys at Osney and Hexham, and priories at Missenden (from where two survivors reached Bodley from Windsor) and at Shelford in Nottinghamshire (whose library is otherwise unattested), Benedictine houses that include Ely cathedral priory, Rochester cathedral priory, Worcester cathedral priory, Chester abbey (already mentioned in connexion with Eton) and Eynsham abbey, and the Cistercian houses of Buildwas and Robertsbridge. The last mentioned had left Robertsbridge early in the fourteenth century, a period when it was used more than once as a *cautio*, and it passed into the hands of Bishop Grandisson of Exeter; one ought to suppose that it was at Exeter cathedral, therefore, before being obtained by the canons of Windsor, but there is a gap in its history.[86] Buildwas has been mentioned already as a house that was alienating books.

The obvious and difficult question is, what are so many books from religious houses doing at Windsor in the fifteenth century? The case of Buildwas may be the most instructive, for we have seen books from Buildwas at the London Carmel, certainly before 1430 and perhaps twenty years before; at Eton, not before its foundation in 1440 but before our list from 1465; and at Windsor from an uncertain date. Ker, as I have quoted, was reluctant to decide whether the Windsor books were to be compared with the large number of ex-monastic books that were sequestered by the Crown and taken to the Royal Library at Westminster between 1528 and 1533, catalogued in 1542 (H2). There is no good evidence to associate their presence at Windsor with King Henry VIII (who tended to put his mark on his books). There is a good case for saying that the house bindings of the Windsor books, imitative of much older bindings, date from the late fifteenth century. Willoughby argued from the availability of ex-monastic books on the market in the early fifteenth century that Windsor's acquisitions, like those of Eton, were picked up in the medieval second-hand trade.[87]

If we patiently work through the evidence, including the books in the university colleges, we can find a good number of ex-monastic books migrating in the fifteenth century, from houses which we would not expect to be losing books; but it is difficult to contextualize that migration. Individual examples add religious houses that lost or sold a book, but it has proved impossible to gather a meaningful cluster better than the case of Buildwas to inform a sense that there was a substantial deaccessioning, and that leaves us in a poor way when it comes to explaining the old homes.

When the focus turns to the new homes, where the evidence is much better, different patterns emerge. Thomas Netter was picking up books as opportunity allowed to augment the holdings of the London Carmel, which was already a substantial library by the 1390s when Robert Ivory died. We have no idea how much Netter bought. Anne Hudson's judgement on the evidence of Netter's *Doctrinale fidei ecclesiae*, 'an immense work of scholarship', was 'that its author had access to an enormous library, most of it presumably at the London Whitefriars'.[88] Sadly, as with almost everything to do with mendicant libraries, we lack the evidence we want.

Eton, by contrast, was a new library, claiming to find difficulty in buying books, and apparently building a library in the first instance through the second-hand trade, which clearly included former monastic books. The canons of Windsor appear to have approached their own collection development in the same way, obtaining books from a very diverse range of institutions around the country. It may be presumed that there was some centralization in the trade and that books from different parts of the country might come to London to be remarketed by men such as John Pye, the stationer.

There were other new libraries established in the fifteenth century. Syon Abbey, founded in 1417, has already been mentioned as a place where the brethren built a considerable library within thirty or forty years, largely through gift by men who became brethren. From the library of Syon, which had grown very large by the early sixteenth century, we appear to have more than one hundred survivors, but Vincent Gillespie has warned that not all of these derive from the brethren's library.[89] Some, not mentioned at all in the existing catalogue, must have reached us from the sisters' library, which Ker made no attempt to separate out. Among the hundred and more survivors, fewer than ten were written before the fifteenth century, and the great majority were current books at the time of acquisition over the course of the fifteenth and early sixteenth century. It is no surprise, when we consider how active was the production of manuscripts in the fifteenth century, that an appropriate library could be built up without evident difficulty from new books.

Archbishop Chichele's foundation of All Souls College in Oxford was established in 1438, after Syon and before Eton, and here too former monastic books were acquired. MS. 12, for example, belonged to one of the Cistercian houses named Stonely, Stoneleigh or Stanley, but it was already in Chichele's possession in 1400. So the escape of monastic books into the second-hand trade must be pushed earlier than the fifteenth century. MS. 82, a twelfth-century Virgil, was at Cirencester abbey in the late thirteenth century but it came to All Souls from Henry Penwortham, Chichele's treasurer, who died while the college was first building. MS. 49, a thirteenth-century copy of the first part of the Digest, was at Bury St Edmunds in the fourteenth century, when it received the letter mark L for *leges* and the number 289. Its front leaves bear marks of chaining, but its late-fifteenth-century binding does not. The guess, therefore, must be that it was chained in Abbot Curteys' library at Bury around 1420 but later in the century was judged surplus to requirements, lost its chains, and headed for Oxford (very possibly via London).

It would be possible to go systematically through libraries established in the fifteenth century and, first, decide whether they were built on modern purchases or on the acquisition of old books or a mixture of the two, and, second, consider whether or not the old books betray evidence of institutional use. There must always have been a second-hand trade to help individuals collect books of an earlier generation, and library books could easily be absorbed into that trade. It would be possible, for example, to go through the several collections of books formed by Bishop William Reed of Chichester in the late fourteenth century, who gave books in substantial numbers to several colleges, to detect whether he was buying up older books as well as paying for the writing of new ones.[90] But finding library books in the second-hand trade is a late phenomenon, which one would not seek to push back much before the late fourteenth century. The unanswered questions remain: Why deaccession? In what circumstances?

There is earlier evidence of books that migrated from one home to another, but it is difficult to track down. Some of it involves very old books, ninth or tenth century, that may have had some special interest. Accidents of exchange could happen. Bury St Edmunds ended up in possession of an interesting set of notes on thirteenth-century Bible lectures from Paris which had been deposited with them by Robert Grosseteste when he borrowed a book and never returned it.[91] On the whole, institutions were not careless, although one does occasionally find complaints about improper loans outside a community. In the 1240s the prior of Christ Church sent two monks to Anglesey priory to demand the return of a single book lent some time before to the rector of Terrington, a mission in which they were successful, for the book was listed in the catalogue in 1326.[92] In another case, visitors at Eynsham abbey complained that the abbot in 1360 had allowed many such loans: he admitted to lending books but he denied doing so improperly.[93] At Canterbury cathedral in 1337 lists were drawn up of some 93 books not in place.[94] From the two *demonstrationes*, in the former slype, by now the main book store between the chapter house and the south transept, 13 were missing from the first and 6 from the second, but the loan notes existed, and members of the community were to answer for them. A further 19 books entered *in paruis tabulis* were also to be answered for. There were a further 38 books signed out in the names of deceased monks. And 17 books were on loan to borrowers outside the community, first among them the Life of St Thomas, signed out to King Edward II (who had been dead for nine years), and last a work attributed to St John Chrysostom, loaned by the king's command.

This rare information is not evidence of casual losses, and records of loss are in fact very infrequent. Deaccession records as such simply do not exist apart from the remarkable and unintentional case of Syon Abbey, where the entries for 282 books were deleted from the catalogue and the shelfmarks reassigned to other, and mostly newer, books. But that was after 1520, when there was a large flow of printed books into the library. Deaccessioned manuscripts at that period, as we shall see in the final chapter, were unlikely to go into the second-hand book trade. They became for the most part scrap parchment.

It is often assumed that university students were a drain on the books of religious houses. Away from abbey, priory or friary, though ostensibly tied to an associated community in Oxford or Cambridge, they spent too much money and ended up pledging books that were never recovered.[95] It may explain some obscure moves. For example, Rewley abbey, outside the west gate of Oxford and close to Osney abbey, was a Cistercian house that makes very little impact on university sources. The only book known from there is now Oxford, Trinity College, MS. 59, a copy of Augustine's *City of God*, written about 1300, which is reported in Br. John Whitfield's detailed catalogue of the library at Dover priory in 1389. In the book an inscription tells that in 1504 it belonged to Rewley and was worth 3/6 (a small sum for a big book). The new catalogue of the manuscripts at Trinity reinterprets what can be seen of the inscription to move the book to Kirkstead, a Cistercian house in Lincolnshire: I am not persuaded by the reading itself (which hinges on the interpretation of an initial *R* or *K*), and I think it impossible to explain such a migration.[96] A drift to Oxford, washing up in Rewley abbey, which by 1504 did not admit students at the university, is on the other hand just possible. We need only suppose that it came up with a monk of Dover.

College libraries experienced a considerable turnover, losing and acquiring books over time, but the books going out and coming in were often the same texts. Fellows of colleges were often, indeed normally, reading the same texts, and, provided that the turnover did not leave too much need unmet, it was not a grave problem. But between our documentary records and our provenanced books, it is very difficult to maintain a picture of books over time. If we simply allow the assumption that once in the library, a book was always in the library, it reduces the difficulty; but it is a fact that books left libraries, sometimes for other libraries, and sometimes for private ownership, perhaps followed by return to another library. The continuing usefulness of twelfth-, thirteenth- and fourteenth-century books in the fifteenth century is not in itself surprising, but it does seem quite surprising that a late-fifteenth-century librarian such as Br. William Charite at Leicester abbey should have been buying, for example, a late-twelfth-century copy of Ovid. He could have got a more recent one, or a printed one. If old books lost their relevance in one context, some at least found new relevance in a different context.

For the most part, college libraries, well attested by surviving books and documents, were there to meet well-defined needs, and we do not expect to find books that have nothing to do with the curriculum or with the careers envisaged by fellows of the college. In the fifteenth century, however, we do find readers with more exotic interests, such as Thomas Gascoigne, who took a great interest in obsolete books and read many, leaving us a trail in his notes.[97] He died in 1458. In the next generation or two, men such as John Gygour appear to have been interested in collecting old books. He was a foundation fellow of All Souls in 1437, moving in the following year to the greater comfort of Merton, where he remained for fifteen years, and he died at a great age on the foundation of Lord Treasurer Cromwell's collegiate foundation at Tattershall (Lincs.) in 1504.[98] He gave books to both Merton and Tattershall, and among those given to Merton was an early-twelfth-century copy of Bede on Proverbs, and other commentaries on various of the *libri sapientiales* in the Old Testament, MS. 181; the scribes of this book include three identified elsewhere as writing books for use by William of Malmesbury – the catalogue makes an assumption and refers to them as Malmesbury monks – along with a dozen not so identified but clearly writing together.[99] A binding leaf shows William of Malmesbury's own formal hand, discarded from a copy of Rufinus. The book has the pressmark of Malmesbury from the fourteenth century, and in the middle of the fifteenth century it was valued at 30 shillings by an Oxford stationer, John Godsond. Soon afterwards it was in the hands of John Gygour, who in 1486 gave it to Merton. This was hardly a useful book in the university context, but it seems to have been deaccessioned from Malmesbury and sent to Oxford before 1458. Gygour cannot have recognized the connexion with William of Malmesbury, which indeed need not have held any interest for him, but he gave it to the college, where it could expect hardly any readers. Another of his books was a four-volume set of the *Pantheologus* of Peter of Cornwall, written by professional scribes in London in 1189 for the author: this was the presentation set for the dedicatee of the first part, Ralph de Alta Ripa, archdeacon of Colchester. It is my belief that Peter had a copy made for himself and four copies for the dedicatees, at least.[100] The work itself is something in the region of 900,000 words. Four scribes worked on part one of the first volume, which is in Merton. By simple multiplication, that would suggest ninety-six scribes copying a minimum number of copies of the *Pantheologus*, for Peter of Cornwall, who was based in London. It is unlikely that anyone in Oxford had heard of Peter of Cornwall at Gygour's date, and unlikely that anyone would take an interest. There is no clue as to where these four volumes had been since Ralph himself left England for the Third Crusade, but they survived for three centuries, and Gygour gave them to Merton as a safe home for what could perhaps be described as antiquarian books in his day.

They would presumably not have been so accessible to the curious had they gone to a monastic library. Unless these volumes had been saved undetectably in some library, perhaps somewhere in London, where Peter of Cornwall was based, they must have changed hands many times and yet survived. They bear an important witness to the London craft in the late twelfth century.

FIVE

Growth, Competition, Stability, Loss, Renewal

THE TITLE OF THIS CHAPTER uses five nouns which characterize libraries at different periods. It is as well to bear in mind the sense of fluidity they convey. The preceding discussion of Neil Ker's *Medieval Libraries of Great Britain* placed some emphasis on the work's tendency to flatten time, inviting a cumulative reading of accession according to date of writing. In highlighting the evidence that religious houses deaccessioned books, which went into the second-hand market and in some cases to other libraries, further emphasis was laid on the role of change in the history of libraries, especially in the fifteenth century. Change over time is no surprise, but it can be easily overlooked, especially when medievalists tend to specialize in a period or an approach. This chapter will offer a survey of the ups and downs of libraries over the five hundred or so years from our earliest booklists to the invention of printing in the fifteenth century. The ups and downs of different libraries, and different types of library, were not synchronized: there is no single curve of growth, setback, renewal, extinction.

The flattening effect of *MLGB* is at its most dangerous with very old books and the libraries to which they are assigned. Anglo-Saxons had not advanced in librarianship to the point of entering *ex libris* inscriptions in books, which became usual only late in the twelfth century. Durham cathedral retains some books that had belonged to the community of St Cuthbert since the late seventh and eighth centuries, which appear under Durham in *MLGB*. Only two appear under Lindisfarne, one of these with a query, and none under Chester-le-Street, where the community spent the better part of a century. It was supposedly at Chester-le-Street, between 934 and 939, that King Athelstan gave five books to the saint.

England's first booklist is a highly questionable document, as quoted, if quoted it is, in the tendentious *Historia de Sancto Cuthberto*; but it tells us that the king gave the community a rich Gospel book, a missal, two more Gospel books, and a copy of the Lives of St Cuthbert in prose and verse.[101] BL MS. Cotton Otho B. IX is a ninth-century Gospel book; its inscriptions recording Athelstan's gift were preserved for us by Humfrey Wanley and destroyed in the Cotton fire of 1731.[102] Cambridge, Corpus Christi College, MS. 183 is primarily a copy of Bede's two Lives of St Cuthbert, dated by Henry Bradshaw to the ninth century and followed in that by M.R. James. But, since Plummer identified the book as that referred to in the *Historia*, it has since been dated on the basis of its being new when Athelstan gave it. Its splendid image of the saint, the king and the book is well known.[103] A church could never have too many Gospel books, and one in a jewelled binding was no doubt a rich gift to honour the saint. But a copy of the two Lives of St Cuthbert can hardly have filled a great deficiency in the library at Chester-le-Street, whose monks' main role had been to protect and preserve the body of St Cuthbert. Do we ask ourselves where the king got these books? A second-hand Gospel book and a new copy of the Lives with a short glossary and lists of bishops. With a picture for the occasion. We have no answer, and few have even speculated.

With the earliest books now at Durham, Ker was, it seems, indecisive. When one turns to the lists under Canterbury cathedral priory or Winchester Old Minster, many entries for pre-Conquest books are marked with queries, and they were often entered on the basis of speculation about origins, not on evidence of provenance, even later medieval provenance. One can understand the reluctance not to exclude books that speak for Anglo-Saxon culture, but it is an area where Ker must be used with special care. He was an Anglo-Saxonist himself who had turned to later medieval bibliography, and he knew that he was lowering the threshold for entry. Anglo-Saxon libraries, however, are a far-off thing, not to be reached on the basis of evidence collected by Ker. Nor are there ninth-century library catalogues such as survive from the Carolingian empire. Michael Lapidge's work on *The Anglo-Saxon Library* created an abstract library in default of evidence for actual libraries. More than half of his book comprises appendices of information, works known to Aldhelm, to Bede, to the writer of the Old English Martyrology (whom Lapidge would go on to identify as Acca of Hexham), and a list of works in manuscripts surviving that were owned somewhere in Anglo-Saxon England, a subject now supported by the extensive listing produced by Lapidge and Gneuss in 2014.[104] There is ample material evidence, and much can be deduced from the quality of penmanship, the evolution of handwriting and the Latin learning of Anglo-Saxon books; but for libraries the evidence simply bears no comparison with that from the twelfth century and later. The books themselves have in most cases lacked the stability that would allow us to work backwards from the later provenance to a more secure mapping of their earlier homes. Continental evidence is not necessarily better marked by early owners, but books have more often come down an organic line of descent that allows us to follow it backwards. This is lacking for England outside Durham.

None the less we have a few booklists. Bishop Æthelwold of Winchester gave books to Peterborough abbey in the second half of the tenth century (BP1). There are 20 titles on the list, distinctly different in culture from the contents of early-twelfth-century libraries, which are much more familiar to us. Not one book survives. Only a quarter of them reappeared in an early-twelfth-century list from Peterborough (BP2), which shows 59 volumes, beginning with newly necessary authors such as Augustine, Jerome, Ambrose, Gregory, but continuing with some authors more popular in pre-Conquest England. It is hard to tell from the list how many of those books remained from the pre-Conquest library. There may have been some out-with-the-old as well as in-with-the-new, but without more of the books themselves it is impossible to know.[105] There exists a real question as to why there are so few surviving books of the eleventh century and earlier in England in comparison with books from the twelfth century onwards. But I am reluctant to hypothesize any significant clearing out, when considerable numbers of pre-Conquest books were retained. The issue may come down to questions of our inability to establish provenance for pre-Conquest books. At Peterborough in the early twelfth century the catalogue includes a book of King Alfred written in English, but its title was not recorded (BP2. 59). (Burton-on-Trent did rather better in listing its half-dozen Old English books in the late twelfth century, B11. 63–69.)

Better than the evidence of Peterborough abbey is that from Exeter cathedral. Two copies of the list of books given to the cathedral by its first bishop, Leofric, in the mid-eleventh century survive, one in Oxford, Bodleian Library, MS. Auct. D. 2. 16, the other removed from the West Saxon Gospels now in Cambridge and prefixed to the Exeter Book of Old English poetry still in Exeter. Leofric moved his episcopal see from Crediton to the town of Exeter in 1050, where he remained bishop beyond the Norman Conquest until his death in 1072. The list represents 66 books, with many entries in English, particularly for the service books, going into Latin for the library books.[106] It was an old-fashioned but by no means obsolete collection. With the lists and with 19 surviving books, the mid-eleventh-century provision at Exeter cathedral is better attested than that for anywhere else in England. It is striking that a number of the books are considered to have come from St Augustine's abbey in Canterbury.[107] Frank Barlow, a fine historian in his generation, betrays an old habit of thinking in his *ODNB* biography of Leofric: 'In the league table of pre-twelfth-century manuscripts, the Exeter scriptorium comes fourth, after Canterbury, Salisbury, and Worcester.' Barlow was in line with his peers in still thinking that the scriptorium was the right way to consider the collection. But the Exeter collection must have come together from a variety of sources.[108] The business will get a new appraisal from James Willoughby in the volume of the Corpus on the library catalogues of the secular cathedrals. Later medieval booklists and a continuing record of good survival, including many volumes now in the Bodleian, have meant that one can also see the expansion of the library under Leofric's successor, the long-serving Norman bishop Osbern FitzOsbern (d. 1103). It is another very striking fact that books acquired by Bishop Osbern, such as Oxford, Bodleian Library, MS. Bodl. 301, are in the hand of a scribe who also worked on books commissioned by Bishop William of Durham in the same period. Bishop William's gifts to the cathedral are well attested and form an important witness to the Normanization of libraries in England. And Durham, it must be remembered, was still a secular chapter during most of Bishop William's time. Monks were introduced only in 1093. Some of the books surviving from Exeter and Durham can be traced back to Bayeux in Normandy, where there were both scribes and exemplars to supply new books.[109]

The evidence for the twelfth century is abundant and well known. Not only can we see the modernization in the libraries at Exeter and Durham but we can see a major period of collection-building around the country, with very good survival of books from, to name a few famous names, Canterbury Christ Church, Bury St Edmunds and St

Albans. There is also important evidence provided by twelfth-century catalogues from the cathedral priories of Rochester, Canterbury and Durham, and we are so well provided that we can describe a new intellectual agenda driving the expansion of libraries in England and in Normandy in the first half of the twelfth century, an agenda centred on study of the Bible and the Latin Fathers.[110] It is, however, predominantly attested in England by Benedictine foundations, and I have warned that too much focus on the Benedictines and their books can lead us to overlook the extensive book economy that provided for the needs of the secular clergy and unknown others. When abbots hired scribes to provide new books for their libraries, and at St Albans gave them lunch as part of the bargain, there must obviously have been a large market for book production outside the abbeys. It has too often been overlooked. Books associated with William of Malmesbury often show the handwriting of scribes who worked for him over considerable periods of time, whether at base in Malmesbury or during his text-hunting tours of religious houses around the country, where he could find books containing works not part of the new agenda but left from the old, and where these scribes made copies at his direction.[111] William's assistants were more likely hired scribes than his monastic brethren. The book, which is MS. 181 mentioned above, given to Merton in 1486, shows more than a dozen hands at work.

The half-century or so of planned collection development in Benedictine abbeys faded out around 1160, its last phase concerned more with law books than with the new theology. From then on, for the most part, abbeys sat on their laurels, satisfied with adequately stocked libraries and growing mostly through haphazard acquisitions by members of the community, referred to as donors, when their books became part of the common stock after the individual owners died. Some houses kept a record of acquisitions paid for by successive abbots, which presumably reflect corporate purchases, but for most institutions the donor was central, the individual monks who acquired a few or many books, indifferent books or important books, and whose souls were prayed for by their successors who read the books. Learning among the Benedictines did not die out, but their libraries entered a long period of passivity.

One has the impression that Cistercian books of high quality are out of synch with the great expansion of Benedictine libraries. Given the date of the order's foundation in 1098, their books date more from the second half of the twelfth century and into the early thirteenth century. England's earliest Cistercian lists are both from Rievaulx (Yorks. NR), around 1190 and 1200, each with upwards of 200 books, and from Flaxley (Glos.), a decade or so later, a smaller library of some 80 books. But the visual quality of books produced for the Cistercians of, say, Byland (Yorks. NR) or Buildwas (Salop) is impressive, and our delight in the elaborate single-colour initials of Cistercian books is increased because such books are rare. We have no evidence of any major Cistercian library in England – though the 400 books from Meaux (Yorks. ER) in the 1390s is not insignificant, and it was not a premier abbey of the order – and as far as Cistercian writers are concerned, there are few indeed between Ralph of Coggeshall, during the reign of King John, and those visible at the end of the fourteenth century. Cistercian obscurity goes beyond passivity.[112]

For the Augustinians we have one clear example of a significant cluster of books from the twelfth century, Llanthony (Glos.), with some ninety surviving manuscripts datable from the twelfth century broadly to the beginning of the thirteenth century. It would be a slow task to examine them to decide whether here there was any detectable change of plan around 1160, between a foundation collection and more haphazard accession, but my suspicion is there was not. There may not have been the widespread expansion in the first half of the twelfth century but there was not an obvious slow-down in the second half. The foundation dates of Augustinian houses, many in the 1120s and 1130s, in any case mean that they started behind the Benedictines, they had less surplus resources to spend on collection development, and they were not directed towards study by their rule. We do not notice the shift towards donors in books belonging to the Augustinians, though donations could play a part. Two lists, both of the end of the twelfth century, from Waltham abbey (Essex) and from Bridlington priory (Yorks. ER), show around 120 books at each (A4, A38). Do we infer that at this date Augustinian libraries were typically so much smaller than major Benedictine libraries? Probably so. Llanthony's library, at its mid-fourteenth-century peak, had some 500 books, including the substantial bequest of 56 books from John Lecche, rather more of which appear as secondary entries added to the catalogue than were cross-matched when the edition was published in 1998 (A16). While 500 is a very decent size, it does not compare with the big Benedictine holdings around the same date, 1350 to 1360. (Size, of course, is a crude means of grading when one acknowledges the number of duplicate copies of the same works; but worse would be to devise a points scheme for appraising overall quality.) How Llanthony would compare with other significant Augustinian collections over the early part of this period we have not the means to say. St Frideswide's and Osney had the advantage of proximity to Oxford; Cirencester (Glos.) seems to have had a flourishing library in the time of its prolific author Alexander Nequam; but the Augustinian library I most wish for evidence from is Holy Trinity in Aldgate, close to the minster of St Martin-le-Grand and not far from the cathedral of St Paul in London. Neither the friars who compiled *Registrum Anglie* nor John Leland in the 1530s visited Holy Trinity, and *MLGB* records all of five books now surviving. The priory had been wealthy, but it was dissolved voluntarily in 1532, seeking the king's help with its corporate debt; it was a harbinger of the dissolution to come, and the fate of the priory's library is unknown.

It was, however, the base from 1170 to 1221 of Peter of Cornwall, prior of the house from 1197. His books have already been mentioned as something of real interest. His *Liber reuelationum*, dated 1200, survives as a primary copy made for the author. It was copied professionally for him.[113] The first book is the work of scribe A; the second book was started by scribe B, who found that he had much more to copy than his colleague. He needed assistance, and scribe C was hired. The chapters were not numbered before copying, and a guess was made: scribe C started a new quire at chapter 600, and when scribe B caught up with him, finishing chapter 582, scribe C was let go and scribe B resumed at chapter 799. Quiring and the gap in the chapter numbers show what was happening. We can see that scribe C was hired at a time when scribe A was sixty folios into his work. They were copying from piles of books, copying only the marked excerpts for inclusion in the new work, though the selection of excerpts was sometimes extensive.

We cannot work out how many books were needed to provide these excerpts, but the assumption would usually be made that they were all available in the library of Holy Trinity. Many would have supposed the scribes to be themselves canons, but this would seem very unlikely. One might also question whether the exempla were all from the priory's library. In London there were other religious houses, and there were scribes for hire. Although we have no known reference to stationers before 1262 (Roger of Oxford, mentioned above), there may well have been stationers in London able to supply exemplars as well as scribes. After all, 1262 is approximately the beginning of that kind of archival evidence, not necessarily the beginning of stationers. Where in London in 1200 would one most likely find a copy of Reginald's Life and Miracles of St Godric, much excerpted by Peter? The extant copies are all associated with Durham cathedral priory.[114] Had Peter borrowed a copy from the London home of Philip of Poitou, bishop of Durham? Or from a London religious house? Or from a stationer?

The scale of the trade has already been alluded to. Peter finished his vast *Pantheologus* in 1189, and had the dedication copy given to the patron of the first part, Ralph de Alta Ripa, who was thanked for paying for the hire of scribes. In the lower margins of Merton College, MS. 191, we find that scribes signed their quires, presumably as part of the reckoning of charges. Does that already imply payment by the quire rather than by the day? Four scribes worked on that book, volume one of four; if we multiply up for three or four volumes and a minimum of five copies, we should be looking at scores of scribes employed at the same time unless production was staggered. With getting on for a million words to each copy, this was an expensive task, and the compilation behind it had also included much making of excerpts. But the aim seemed to have been to get it done. It is small wonder that Peter was grateful to his patrons who had paid for the scribes. (Later, as prior, he might have done without such external support.) The number of professional scribes available in London must have been capable of taking on a task of this size, and, one may suppose, doing so without disrupting more regular work. I incline to think that in London the trade and the established libraries, about which we know so little, would have cooperated, but there remains a distinct possibility that the trade kept exemplars of popular texts even at this relatively early date.

Would it be surprising if London was already, and had been for a long time, the centre of the book economy in England? It would not be surprising. There is a leading passage, to be used with caution, in Thomas of Marlborough's account of the abbots of Evesham, written about 1216 but much of it based on the work of Dominic of Evesham. (The passage is probably in Thomas of Marlborough's words rather than Dominic of Evesham's.) It concerns Abbot Ælfweard, towards the end of Cnut's reign, who retained the abbacy of Evesham upon becoming bishop of London and who bought relics stolen from Flanders and a quantity of books:

> Idem uero Æiluuardus episcopus et abbas sanctissimas corporis reliquias fere omnes beati Odulfi confessoris a mercatoribus eas Londonias portantibus mercatus est digno pretio, id est centum marcis, atque ad istum locum quem maxime dilexerat transmisit laudabiliter reseruandas hic perpetuo. Libros etiam plurimos tam diuinos quam gramaticos de Londonia transmisit.
>
> [The same Ælfweard, bishop and abbot, bought for a noble price, namely one hundred marks, almost all the relics of blessed Odulf the Confessor from the merchants who had brought them to London, and he sent them to the place he most loved to be praiseworthily kept here for ever. He also sent from London a very large number of books both service books and school books.][115]

It is not that Ælfweard is creating an important library for scholarship: he is rather meeting basic needs, albeit on a plentiful scale. But he is not hiring scribes or directing his monks: he is buying books seemingly in the trade in 1034 or soon after. Our immediate source is writing around 1216. If we doubt his knowing the actuality from Cnut's reign, that is still very early evidence for trade supply.

From the 1230s onwards we start to see direct evidence of the book trade, craft workshops like that of William de Brailes in Oxford, along Catte Street, attested both by its books and by record sources for the occupancy of shop premises.[116] From then on, continually if not continuously, art-historical work has built a picture of workshops characterized by style or by individual artists, and no one is likely to challenge the notion that in London and Oxford, and perhaps other places, we have an answer to the supply-side question. The question of exemplars for texts remains problematic. In the universities there was provision by the end of the thirteenth century, and perhaps earlier, for the supply of approved books, but many works spread and circulated that were not on the university curriculum.[117] We know that libraries could not have been self-sufficient in the provision of exemplars, but we do not know how works were made available to meet what may have been only occasional need.

From the second quarter of the thirteenth century we must include a new kind of consumer of library books, the friars. We know them as studious, though some medieval authors made them an object of satire. Not all friars were alike. In Oxford, in Cambridge, in Paris, and across Europe friars were prodigious consumers, authors and distributors of books. I name only Thomas Aquinas, Bonaventure and the Oxford teacher from Tweeddale, John Duns Scotus. It must be a cause of great regret that the evidence from the English friaries is so poor. One suspects that there was much more than has survived. Their motivation in creating *Registrum Anglie* was a desire to read everything that mattered, and one may imagine that they sought to make copies. The fact that Bishop Grosseteste's books went to the Grey Friars in Oxford to serve as exemplars for the future as early as 1253 is a sign that the bishop saw it as a serious research library.[118] It is almost all gone without leaving a meaningful trace. We have a handful of books older than the Grey Friars' foundation, a few thirteenth-century books, a few from the fourteenth century, and some later items, no consistent *ex libris* at any period, no shelfmarks (though Franciscans elsewhere used simple shelfmarks) and no documentary evidence.

Friars personally were not bound by stability as Benedictines were. Ker complained of the difficulty of dealing with books marked only with the names of individual friars. Were their houses unable to provide stability for their books? By the time John Leland gained entry to the Oxford Grey Friars in 1535, he found a library room full of dust, spiders, and the grubs and beetles of cliché, with not a lot of books to attract his interest.[119] The library had changed much over time: that library room had been built at some high point of interest; its books had drifted away. We have to look back over several phases of change to try to imagine what the library of the Grey Friars in Oxford looked like in 1253. Were friars too much users of books to maintain a safe library of deposit? Where a Benedictine house might have space to leave hundreds of books unused for a century or two, friars had more use for the books and less luxury of storage space.[120]

In the 1320s it may be that at Thorney abbey (Cambs.) we can see an extreme outcome of that Benedictine passivity. A scrap of parchment used by the precentor of Thorney over a period of years to track the annual distribution of books to the monks on the first Monday of Lent survived in the binding of the Tanner Bede. One is able to read the entries for four non-consecutive years between 1324 and 1330, and to provide a plausible reconstruction of monastic seniority in order to track which books each monk took over time.[121] Three things emerged from that exercise: a surprising number of monks were absentees on this occasion laid down in the Rule for the distribution of the books; many monks read only the most basic material; and a small supply of books provided for the needs of the Lenten distribution year after year. One of those books is now Oxford, Bodleian Library, MS. Bodl. 680, a miscellany of medical works, written in the thirteenth century and given to the abbey by Ralph Newton, clerk. The impossible question is whether there was besides these books a large and neglected library of books built up first in the early twelfth century and added to by individual monks over the succeeding years. If not, what had happened to it? By the mid-1340s we know that the monks had some racy book that circulated among them, condemned by the bishop but slow to be eradicated.[122] It was perhaps a French fabliau, but it is not great evidence for the abbey as a community of readers with what should have been a mature library.

The 1320s were perhaps a nadir for the Benedictines, but not for all of them. From 1336 Pope Benedict XII wanted a revival of Benedictine learning and enjoined larger communities to maintain one or two monks at university.[123] Before taking this to be an outside imposition on monks who had abandoned their books, it might be remembered that the very large Eastry catalogue of 1,800 books at Canterbury dates from 1326, that the very large Ramsey catalogue probably dates from the 1330s. There was interest, there was even learning, but the pope's aim was to spread best practice more widely in the order. Within England one might think of John of London (*fl. c.* 1290–*c.* 1330), monk of St Augustine's abbey: if one could see the huge and complex library catalogue of that abbey in accession order, like those of Canterbury and Ramsey, under the name of John of London would be more books than came from any other donor, among them a quantity of serious material in mathematics and astronomy. Yet we do not have any work of learning from this John of London, despite attempts to link him with others of the same name in the thirteenth century and later in the fourteenth.[124]

Another name which might enter the discussion at this point is Ranulf Higden, monk of Chester, who from the beginning of Edward III's reign began to circulate a very successful universal chronicle, which he continued to revise until his death at an advanced age in 1364. He outlines his major sources in the preface, but from time to time as one reads him one finds that he quotes some really unexpected sources. His use of the tract *De situ Albanie* and other rare Scottish sources is just one example.[125] We know little enough about the library at Chester, and I doubt we should describe its contents on the basis of Higden's reading, but he is an example of a very successful Benedictine reader, author and publisher at a time when one does not expect it. One must wonder whether he was permitted to spend a lot of his time in London.

It has already been argued here that the late fourteenth century was the apogee of medieval library catalogues in England, as much for their handling of complex metadata as for the size of the collections described. Much of this was the product of slow accumulation, but it came with renewed interest, and in the mid- to late fourteenth century we may see a surge in expansion again. The librarians who gave us some of these catalogues, in particular Henry of Kirkestede and John Whitfield, commissioned and wrote books, having concern for their libraries. And over the next generation or two we see the selection of books and the building of library rooms equipped with reading desks for more concerted study away from the activity of the cloister walk. Bury and Canterbury, for example, had such libraries, and so, it may be suspected, did a fair number of other places. The evidence can be thin: evidence of chaining on surviving books or mention in accounts of money spent on chains and locks serve as pointers to the establishment of a library room with desks. A room with fifty desks and some 750 books may be inferred from the system of shelfmarks revealed in an index catalogue from St Mary's abbey in York (B120), a big conclusion from such evidence. Now for the first time, at the end of the fourteenth and in the early fifteenth century, a connexion becomes visible between the books that have reached us and the late medieval library furniture that we know from rare survivals. This visible connexion has made the chained library a widely perceived realization of the medieval library.[126]

English Benedictine evidence reached its zenith in the late fourteenth century, and it is much more difficult to follow even Benedictine libraries into the fifteenth century, although we know that the number of books produced in England was increasing at the time. The library catalogue of St Augustine's abbey in Canterbury provides a challenging tool because underneath the fifteenth-century transcription there lies the late-fourteenth-century catalogue much augmented, no doubt by many hands, with all the accessions of a hundred years.[127] If we only had the original to study and not a later copy! The simple fact is that in the fifteenth century our attention shifts again away from the Benedictines and we allow them again, without strong warrant, to fall into torpor.

The evidence, mentioned above, of accessions to the London Carmel in the late fourteenth and early fifteenth centuries and the extraordinary catalogue from the Austin Hermits in York, in 1372, and with the addition of Br. John Argam's 300 books shortly afterwards, stand to show that the friars might have been very active at this time. But there is simply not the evidence to show it. Yet by the time that the Benedictines in Bury and York were equipping their library rooms, and perhaps selling off surplus books, there were other houses that were definitely deaccessioning on some scale, to the advantage of individuals buying books, who were happy to acquire old books, and even old works, long forgotten in some cases, and to seek to preserve them. This was to the advantage of some new libraries, such as those of the canons of Windsor and the fellows of Eton.

It should also be remembered that the universities had come into existence long before the fifteenth century. The early evidence from Oxford of Master Theobald of Étampes as a teacher around 1100 is perhaps not well known, but Gerald of Wales's reading to the scholars in 1189 is widely familiar.[128] Oxford had a chancellor from 1208, Cambridge a little later. The thirteenth century saw the foundation of the first colleges both in Oxford and in Cambridge and the first documentary evidence of the local book trade. Yet the first substantial evidence of college libraries is from 1318 × 1334, the catalogue of eighty-seven volumes of arts books at Merton College (UO46). The same college was the beneficiary of an earlier testament leaving two books in 1300 (UO115). From the 1330s testaments increase in numbers thick and fast, but college catalogues are few for the remainder of the century. The flood of documentation is not easily digested into a clear sense of library holdings, though it does paint a lively picture of fellows borrowing college books and, later in life, remembering their successors in the disposal of their personal libraries.

When indexed by author and title, it is possible to see clearly enough the works most in demand. It was suggested in the previous chapter that Merton, one of the best evidenced college libraries, was losing copies of necessary books and replacing them without our really noticing in the evidence as currently analysed. The citations of the *secundo folio* demand more attention. With 33 documents for Merton in the Oxford volume of the Corpus and 344 recognized survivors from the medieval college, it is still impossible to say how many there were when the medieval holdings reached their peak. After inventories of arts books and theology books at different points in the fourteenth century, there is no further inventory. We may allow that the record of annual loans will reflect the great majority of the collection, but even here the evidence is suboptimal. There survive five arts lists of loans, and two theology lists, and there is no year when both lists are known. The earliest is 1372, the latest 1519, and we may reasonably suppose that such annual loans had been recorded since well before 1372. So, out of a potential of (say) four hundred annual records, seven exist. These are transient, throwaway documents, redundant within a year if all the fellows had behaved well or within a few if some did not return their books promptly. We must be thankful for what we have. By putting together lists from 1452 and 1519, we might hazard a total of some 700 books, but that lapse of time saw so much change in the book economy that we should hesitate. The loan list from 1519 (UO66) is a challenging document, listing no more than the *secundo folio* for 442 volumes of theology. How many of these represent recent expansion in the collection with printed books? That is a very hard question to answer. It is difficult enough to match a *secundo folio* to pre-1501 editions, more than difficult after 1500, so that one can hardly form a meaningful picture from such a list.[129]

The late fourteenth and fifteenth centuries had also seen the foundation of some rich collegiate churches. A few were blessed with continuity in the sixteenth century, like the university colleges and unlike the religious houses, so that from Windsor, Eton and Winchester we have still enough books to see their libraries built from manuscripts acquired through the second-hand trade.[130] The new abbey at Syon grew largely through new books and was acquiring printed books at an early date, as the index of imprints in Vincent Gillespie's edition makes clear at a glance.[131] What should also be mentioned is the increasing visibility of professional books for lawyers and physicians in the fifteenth century and private books for personal devotions, and of strong record evidence for a book trade from the late fourteenth century continuously into the sixteenth century and after, massively centred in London.[132]

In the long run it would be hard to say that libraries as a sector in the book economy kept apace with the private sector. In part that is because for the latter we are poorly apprised of its early history. For the Anglo-Saxon period, it is almost assumed that a book is an institutional book, though I doubt the truth of that. Our first private booklist names the works in the library of a man named Athelstan around the end of the tenth century, written into a manuscript that subsequently came into the library of St Augustine's abbey in Canterbury (BA1. 434). We infer he was a schoolmaster from the books he owned; it was a modest collection.[133] Richard, parson successively of St Martin in the Cornmarket in Worcester and the suburban church of Tibberton, and rural dean of Worcester, in 1221 had the misfortune to have two cartloads of his books detained by a toll-gatherer at Wychbold, ten miles out of town. How many books make two cartloads and what part of his personal library this represents are unclear, and we have no idea why they were on the road, but the toll-collector was accused of misconduct and the case entered the legal records.[134] It is probably the largest private library attested so early in England, yet the parson is an unknown but surely not untypical figure.[135] We could do much more to track personal books over time, and, so equipped with data, we might have less sense of major change in the proportion of the library sector within the wider book economy.

SIX

Decay and Closure of Libraries

THE DISSOLUTION OF THE MONASTERIES plays a large role in perceptions of medieval libraries and has done since students began to think about the subject. Ker indicated in the first edition of *MLGB* in 1941 that 'the limit of date is about 1540 for English and Welsh libraries and a decade or two later for Scotch libraries. Books with inscriptions, &c., dating from the period of the Marian revival are not listed.' He had not mentioned dissolution, but Queen Mary did not revive medieval libraries; she revived a handful of monasteries. The mere mention of '1540' and the dissolution is understood.

Its immediate aftermath *locally* had an important effect on the preservation of books from the dissolved houses, a subject of great interest. As long as *MLGB* was dominated by books from dissolved religious houses, there was a close link between the events of 1536 to 1540 and the listing of what survived the wreck.[136] The dissolution has had the blame for our loss of countless medieval books that might otherwise have survived, but our dashed hopes must be qualified. Nigel Ramsay in an essay on the break-up of English libraries in the sixteenth century spelt out reasons why the dissolution came at the worst possible time for libraries, which were struggling to survive anyway.[137] The dissolution had only indirect impact on the universities. The religious houses in Oxford and Cambridge disappeared, including the Benedictine colleges in Oxford, but there was no eager takeover of their books by neighbouring colleges. Canterbury College ceased to exist when its parent body, the cathedral priory, surrendered, and there was no thought of its continuance in relation to the cathedral refounded as a secular chapter.[138] Its recognizable books – that is, medieval manuscripts from the cathedral that had been assigned to the college – were well represented among leaves used by Oxford binders to bind modern printed books.[139]

In Cambridge the university library was, in effect, abandoned in 1546–7. Being found to be of no use to anyone, the space was converted into a theology lecture room. No money was spent on books for the university library between 1530 and 1573.[140] In Oxford, the university library faded away in the same period. Protestant reformers cleared the desks of books, and in January 1556 even the furniture was sold off. The desks and benches were bought by Richard Marshall, dean of Christ Church, to set up his college library in the former monastic refectory of St Frideswide's.[141] Marshall was dean only under Queen Mary, his Catholic views were often to the fore, and he may have wished to create an old-fashioned home for books displaced by more forward-looking heads of colleges – perhaps a rearguard action, therefore, rather than an early sign of recovery for libraries.

There was much more afoot to reduce the role of libraries than the dissolution of the monasteries. The fact that dissolution happened early in England has focused on it a change that was widespread across Europe in the preceding decades. Gerhardt Powitz, in an article entitled '*Libri inutiles*', spoke of a great perishing of books (*Büchersterben*), and also more actively of a great *Zerstörungswerk*, 'a work of destruction'.[142] In countries that escaped the secularization of monasteries at this period the evidence shows that the flood of printed books was accompanied by a large-scale disposal of manuscripts. Powitz puts some emphasis on the need for scrap parchment to bind the flood of new books, and notes also the concurrent rebinding of manuscripts that were retained. But binding leaves are a symptom of destruction: they do not represent the cause. Scrap parchment had a value greater, it seems, than the same parchment as bearer of manuscript text. The cause here was simple obsolescence. The second-hand market that allowed twelfth- and thirteenth-century manuscripts to be sold on had dried up at some point. We identified the example of William Charite's acquiring such books for Leicester around 1480 or 1490, when he might just as well have bought new printed books. Twenty or thirty years later, there is no evidence for keeping the old and ample evidence for the move from manuscript to print.[143]

Two topics therefore run in parallel in the closing years of the fifteenth century and the first decades of the sixteenth century. One is the taking up of printed books in the same institutional settings as had for hundreds of years maintained libraries of manuscripts. In countries where religious houses were not dissolved in the period of the Reformation, this transformation happened and would no doubt have been as well attested in England as in France and Italy if religious houses had survived. It is noticeable in English evidence, but we tend to overlook it, in part because libraries have, since the seventeenth century, separated manuscripts as old and printed books as part of a continuing collection.[144] The practical reason why Ker and his colleagues made no search for printed books that had belonged to institutions before 1540 was, and is, that catalogues of printed books – card catalogues or slip catalogues in guard books – have not usually recorded marks of ownership and that the work involved for Ker might have meant going along library shelves and opening countless sixteenth- and seventeenth-century books in the process of finding those that might be relevant. It was not done, and the evidence is therefore under-recorded because *MLGB* only records printed books with medieval provenances when the compilers happened upon them.

The second topic is the cessation of libraries. The university libraries closed because they were no longer needed. Cathedrals and colleges that enjoyed continuity through the period might retain their old books alongside new books, if they had the space and so pleased. Worcester cathedral priory had kept its library in a part of the church itself, where there was no competition for the space. Other institutions were not so well placed. Libraries disappeared whether the institution closed or remained. Now, this is a phenomenon that might be expected as much on the Continent as in England, but I am not conscious that it has attracted attention, and I am in no position to point to examples. If, as in England, there was a revival after thirty or forty or fifty years, the gap may have been forgotten in places where there was one, especially in countries where monastic institutions simply continued to exist: it would take close attention to say whether accessions had more or less dried up for a few decades while the old books gathered dust until times changed, shelves were rearranged, and new books were acquired.

The reason libraries ceased is because printed books were so much cheaper and so much more easily obtained: those individuals who wanted to read could form their own personal studies in the sixteenth century. If college fellows could buy what they needed with ease, they had less need to depend on the lending of books held by the college for several generations past. They could have copies in the new medium, lighter, cleaner, easier to consult. Over time the need for libraries re-emerged, not because books had reverted to being too expensive but because scholarship sometimes demanded that one consult works no longer available in print or that one compare old and new editions. The accumulation of a third and fourth generation of printed books required libraries, on a scale not seen before, not so much to manage the current availability of a work but to manage availability from generation to generation. The gap between the closure of libraries and the formation of new ones was therefore relatively short. At

Cambridge university library, as mentioned above, new acquisitions ended in 1530, maintenance lapsed in 1546–7, and purchases restarted in 1573. In Oxford the lapse was a little later and the revival came only with Thomas Bodley in 1598. In the meantime, some college libraries were growing apace in the late sixteenth century; Corpus Christi, for example, with its catalogue of 371 books from 1589, making it a rare example of continuity or, at least, of revival after a relatively short break. Although not a medieval college nor a medieval list, this was included in the Corpus volume of medieval catalogues for Oxford (UO33).

Detailed inventories taken at the time of dissolution are not rare, but it is very rare to find their referring to books, which formed no part of the commissioners' brief. William Farrer printed in his edition of the cartulary of Cockersand abbey (Lancs.) an inventory taken two years before the dissolution, which has survived among the rentals and surveys retained in the archive of the Duchy of Lancaster, so not part of the dissolution materials. Two short passages might be highlighted.[145]

First, under the heading 'Ornaments of the Church', we see thirty stalls in the choir, valued at 66*s* 8*d*, far less than they would have cost to make:

Item xxx stalles in the quere there valued by estymacion at lxvj s. viij d.

Item liiij Parchemyn Bookes in the seyd Qyere
valued by estymacion at lxvj s. viij d.

At the time of the surrender in 1539 there were twenty-two canons besides the abbot, so the institution was not too run-down. The next item is 54 parchment books in the choir, valued at the same 66*s* 8*d*. A marginal note says *M. quia nimis*, 'Too much'. A little further on in the account, there is a heading for 'The Librarye', itself an unusual thing to find, and three items are valued:

Item lij Books in the seyd Librarye v s.

Item A wyndowe there cont' by estymacion vj Fotez of glass at ij d. the fote xij d.

Item an Ambury one the Cloysterside wherin ar liiij Bokes pratsed by estymacion at vj s. viij d.

A mere five shillings for 52 books in the library is just over a penny per book in old money. Six feet of glass at tuppence per foot makes one shilling. And another 54 books in the aumbry on the cloister side, *6s 8d*; now that is almost three-halfpence per book in old money, but the rate per book does not seem to matter. The sums are round ones, a quarter and a third of £1. The commissioners' clerk might as well not have counted them, for their individual values are insignificant. It is, however, particularly interesting to see that there was a room designated as a library: it has one window, so this is presumably not a large room fitted out as a reading room with desks. The rest of the books are still in the aumbry on the side of the cloister, where books had presumably been kept since church and cloister were built at the beginning of the thirteenth century. Nothing of this survives now; there is only the chapter house to see. The value of these books is almost trivial, but the parchment books in the choir were valued at more than a shilling apiece. There has to be a reason, and we may guess that these included choirbooks and perhaps some service books. The relatively high value might suggest large-format books. But liturgical books from a Premonstratensian abbey had no second-hand value at all in England at this date, so, guessing still, is this a value based on their scrap value as parchment? That would seem plausible. So the relatively high value may point to large-format books, sheets of parchment big enough to have multiple uses. In a few lines of inventory, we see a library that has modernized, now equipped with a library room and a stock of more than one hundred printed books. (They ought to be taken as printed books, for parchment is not mentioned.) This is a small library for the 1530s, and many an individual would have had more books. It was of insignificant value. And there were parchment books, not necessarily old ones, holding greater value, perhaps, as scrap.

From Monk Bretton near Barnsley in South Yorkshire we have a still more unusual record of 140 books kept by a small group of former monks of the priory, who continued to live a communal life in the reign of Queen Mary (B55). We may wonder whether the making of the list, in 1558, and of the cartulary in which it was written, is a sign of their hoping that Queen Mary would renew communal life at their monastery. The list is concise, in the old style with no second folios, and no place and year of printing as would become the new style of listing. Titles only are listed, but these are sometimes distinctive of title pages from printed books, and there can be little doubt that they were nearly all in print, almost all in Latin. There are a few items in English, all of them printed after 1500. For example, *Kalender of Schepherdes*, of which there were seven London editions known between 1506 and 1528 (and more from 1559 onwards). Most curious in the Monk Bretton list is an entry for *Aurora totam fere bibliam metricis versibus complectens*, which reads like the title from a sixteenth-century edition of the late-twelfth-century work of Petrus Riga, but no edition is known from any date earlier than this list. Might this be a unique attestation from Yorkshire of an edition of an internationally used schoolbook, otherwise lost? Only one work from Monk Bretton appears definitely to be in manuscript, a copy of the *Musica monachorum* of the Yorkshire Carthusian John Norton. Here, it seems, we have evidence for a modest monastic library on the eve of the dissolution, still held in common by four monks who simply kept the books when pensioned twenty years before the list was made.[146] Of course, we cannot swear that there were not also quantities of old manuscripts in the priory, which they chose not to keep: *MLGB* shows only a thirteenth-century Bible and a thirteenth-century breviary, its kalendar Cluniac and associated with nearby Pontefract, which was bought by a monk of Monk Bretton in the early sixteenth century. Was it bought for use or as an old-time curiosity?

Now *MLGB* is a book for medievalists, and the Monk Bretton catalogue is primarily of interest to students of Catholicism on the eve of the Reformation, not to medievalists. Sometimes we see the same attitude reflected in our sources. Jock Liddell, one of the five compilers of the first *MLGB*, edited a list of works noticed by someone touring some of the religious houses of Lincolnshire and picking up books on behalf of the king or perhaps of Cardinal Wolsey.[147] The list had been associated with John Leland, the king's antiquary, who was known to have toured parts of England and to have made such notes of titles – as well as acquiring some of the books themselves for the king's library or for his own personal collection. These lists from Lincolnshire sometimes show a plus sign against a title, and wherever the sign is used the book can usually still be found in the Royal Library. But at no fewer than sixteen houses out of thirty-two, the visitor recorded no titles: these include six houses of friars, five of Augustinian canons, three of Gilbertine canons, one of Premonstratensian canons, and one of Cistercian monks. James Carley has dated this list to the summer of 1528, and the purpose of it was to find books that might aid the king's argument for his divorce from Queen Katharine.[148] Only once is the word *libraria* used, and that at Lincoln cathedral.[149] Where there was nothing worth recording, the visitor wrote, in varying words, that there were books, albeit nothing but common printed books or, occasionally, common or printed books, 'complures libri communes tamen arteque impressoria litteris dediti', 'complures codices sed uel communes arteue impressoria litteris imbuti'. He sometimes says there were printed books or books not to our purpose, which at least implies that they were not printed, 'multi sunt ibidem libri non tamen ad rem pertinentes uel communiter impressi', *commonly printed*. For this visitor, there is a persistent equation between *communis*, usual, commonplace, and printed. So his lack of interest is a signal that these places, most of them minor, had no historic collection but merely recent books, sometimes on a scale sufficient for him to use the word *multi*. It is not what he wanted, but it tells us that small religious houses had modernized by the early sixteenth century. It should not surprise. Only two Benedictine houses were visited on this tour, and the largest number of titles recorded, thirteen, was at Bardney abbey, with two at Frieston, a little cell of Crowland abbey. Such places may also have had their modern collections, but the record focused on older items and does not tell.

The positive evidence for the move into printed books is not often readily accessible, and the best view that we get is at Syon Abbey, where Thomas Betson's large catalogue of the brethren's library from *c.* 1500, with nearly three hundred overwritten entries from *c.* 1524, shows that printed books were being acquired by the brethren from as early as *c.* 1468. Mary Bateson, a good medievalist, remarked in her preface that she embarked on her edition with no sense of the bibliographical challenge involved.[150] She did well, but we now have Gillespie's edition, perhaps the most straightforwardly rewarding volume of the Corpus of British Medieval Library Catalogues, an outstanding catalogue well presented.[151] Some hundreds of early printed editions can be recognized, mostly from their second folios, and the most common source of editions is Cologne, as appears from the index of imprints. The surviving books associated with Syon include a handful still later than 1524, but these are mostly books that belonged to sisters of the abbey. For example, a copy of Richard Whitford's work *The Pype, or Tonne, of the Lyfe of Perfection* (Robert Redman, London, 1532), now Oxford, Bodleian Library, 4° W 2 Th.Seld., belonged to Eleanor Fetyplace, a sister of Syon at the dissolution; a copy of *The Tree and xii. Frutes of the*

Holy Goost (Robert Copman, London, 1535), now Cambridge, Trinity College, C.7.12, belonged to '(Mar^{t}) Windesor Domina de Syon', and another copy, now at Ampleforth, belonged to Dorothe Coderynton, a sister of Syon at the time of its dissolution. A curious pair of books which we may associate with the brethren's library came to Merton College: they are not mentioned in Betson's catalogue. There is a Bible concordance all in Hebrew, printed at Venice in 1524, and a Hebrew grammar printed at Basel in 1525. One carries the name of John Fewterer, sometime fellow of Pembroke College, Cambridge, who appears as donor of 75 books in the Syon Abbey catalogue, the other the name of Bonde, identified with William Bonde, donor of 29 books in the catalogue. Neither of these two books appears in the catalogue. Both men were still very much alive when the catalogue was drawn up: Bonde died in 1530, Fewterer in 1536. Another book, a Latin commentary on the Pauline Epistles, printed at Paris in 1528, now at Stonor Park, is inscribed with the name of John Coppinger, who died in 1538 shortly before the dissolution as a brother at Syon, and also 'Pray for William Bonde and John Copynger, good daughter', suggesting that it had been passed to a family member, possibly a sister of Syon.

Syon was a relatively recent foundation with a relatively up-to-date late-medieval collection of books, and it was clearly moving forwards. Half the library was made up of printed books. A Benedictine house with a large and old library, such as Canterbury cathedral priory, was also acquiring printed books, in this case from *c.*1470, but knowledge of them is close to insignificant, and it is equally thin for any printed books at Canterbury College in Oxford. Although inventories exist from the early sixteenth century, the books were mostly the same as had been there for decades, and those that survive from the college lists are mostly recognized by marks from the priory itself and by association between the priory catalogue and the college inventories. In both universities the evidence for the shift from manuscript to printed books is less apparent than one might wish and expect. The explanation for this is, probably, price. Colleges retained their old collections still at the beginning of the sixteenth century, but fellows were buying books for themselves. An unusual example of a major donation is more than two hundred volumes gifted to Corpus Christi College, Cambridge, 'ad usum magistri et sociorum', by its former master Peter Nobys, after 1525 and perhaps as late as 1542 (UC22). This was a private collection bigger than the communal stock. The college library as such was in abeyance, but when a new library was fitted out in the 1560s – an early renewal – there were then just over one hundred books in the six stalls of the library (UC25). The magnificent gift of Archbishop Parker would transform the college library into a treasure house of old and very old manuscripts, many of them from Canterbury, but that marks a different world, in which medieval books were antiquities. (It has been argued above that the likes of John Gygour thought this way a century earlier, but that did not in itself prevent discontinuity in many college libraries.)

The changes in college libraries are in most cases quite obvious. For two centuries – roughly 1320 to 1520 – these small institutions had used communal resources to provide students and scholars with sufficient books for their studies, but in the early sixteenth century investment in libraries generally ceased. Books chained to desks languished or worse, lending stocks were depleted and not replenished, and old handwritten volumes on parchment fell into the hands of bookbinders, to be used, one or two bifolia at a time, in binding modern books. Readers who needed current texts had no use for manuscripts inherited from the previous generation, let alone from forebears centuries before. Intellectual change, always present, but fast-moving in the early sixteenth century, coincided with the relatively recent medium of print, the convenience of paper, and significantly lower prices, to turn old books into lumber, apparently worth more as scrap than for use. In his catalogue of the few manuscripts held by Clare College, Cambridge, M.R. James emphasized how often it could be said that 'This and that college once possessed a large and interesting library, which has now entirely disappeared.' In another catalogue published in the same year, Christ's, a later foundation, he began: 'The lament over the lost library has to be uttered, as in other cases, so in that of Christ's College.' It was a recurring theme. Peterhouse, Gonville Hall and to some extent Pembroke retain many of their medieval books, but other colleges do not and did not. The same is true in Oxford, where there are more colleges still with numbers of medieval books but in no case a real reflection of the scale of the late-medieval collection. M.R. James did not focus on the circumstances, but the loss generally belongs to the early to mid-sixteenth century, and it was not the result of carelessness, still less the impact of dissolution. It was the result of keeping up to date, and we may ask why some colleges did not clear out their old and useless books. Those that did keep them would find, forty or fifty years later, that they had an advantage in historic collections, and by the beginning of the seventeenth century Thomas James's *Ecloga Oxonio-Cantabrigiensis* (1600) suggests that this was already an advantage to make public. While college libraries had languished, university libraries had closed. That may reflect on the difference in available space or in the domestic presence of a community of fellows.

The libraries of secular cathedrals and of colleges outside the universities rarely fared better, and the dissolution of the Benedictine cathedral priories did not in most cases lead to a rich inheritance of manuscripts by their secular successors. Out of sixteen major medieval houses that survived under new constitutions, Durham and Worcester are the two that stand out as retaining a significant fraction of their medieval books. And, despite the fact that Edward VI's Protestant ministers exhorted deans and chapters to build libraries of books for the study of scripture and Protestant theology, there is little sign that they did so until the second half of the seventeenth century, by which time deans and canons were a good deal more prosperous.[152]

The circumstances of intellectual change, new books in a new medium, and much cheaper availability, together with a sense of looking forward rather than continuing in the old ways, meant that the older libraries were on the way out with or without the dissolution of the monasteries. In England there was no conversion of books to secular use such as happened in Zurich in 1524, no policy of sequestration such as happened in Sweden in 1527–8 (where thousands of books were taken to a former Franciscan convent on an island in Stockholm and kept for decades before it was decided to use them to provide wrappers for the accounts produced by government officials).[153] It is equally true that in England there was no policy of sale or destruction. If pensioned former monks or incoming buyers of monastic buildings did not want the books, anyone could have them, and in some places we can infer that there were men who, for whatever reason, took and kept old books.[154] The colossal dispersion was not always immediate: it has been shown for Canterbury cathedral, which continued as a secular foundation, that books were being removed from the claustral buildings over a period of three generations.[155] That is part of the story of what lies behind *MLGB*, something well treated by Ker in his paper to the Bibliographical Society following the publication of the first edition.[156] The subject of that paper, the migration of monastic manuscripts, reflected that early view of *MLGB* in its formative stages as evidence of what had belonged to religious houses and had survived the dispersion and destruction caused by their dissolution.

But in this book I have urged that we should not think of medieval libraries so much in monastic terms as has been the habit. It was a habit among seventeenth-century antiquaries, and it was reflected in the eighteenth century's sneering view of the Middle Ages as monkish times. But it is misleading. The fourteenth and fifteenth centuries have left us ample evidence that the secular institutions, such as the university colleges, had a large role in the library economy. Their surviving books now entered into *MLGB3* account for 25 per cent of the books listed in the database, several times greater than the percentage in *MLGB2*. If one recalls that there are two universities and thirty-five medieval colleges and halls providing evidence, against some five hundred religious houses, then it becomes clear that in the later Middle Ages there was some concentration of books in just two towns. This concentration is especially true of institutional books. Students needed the loan of books but, as their careers took off, they could afford private studies. The handful of major old libraries of manuscripts around the country were probably making very little difference, and it would perhaps profit us little to wonder how much benefit the monks of Bury St Edmunds drew from the two thousand volumes they had at the peak of their letter-marking system. We have little sense that they were using them, and little sense that they let others in to do so. The making of a library room by Abbot Curteys may have meant an early-fifteenth-century deaccession of surplus books. And in many religious houses the decline in the number of vowed religious over the late fourteenth and fifteenth centuries may have been a factor around the country.

If there is widespread evidence that the secular part of the library economy was stronger than the monastic part in the fourteenth and fifteenth centuries, I have tried also to make a case that we have put too much emphasis on the monastic part in the eleventh and twelfth centuries, forgetting the extent of a secular book economy and ignoring the evidence for London as a commercial centre of the book trades already in the late twelfth century and perhaps even in the early eleventh.

✤

At the outset of this work, three broad points were advertised: that libraries in medieval England (and everywhere else) took many forms, such that the abstract Medieval Library is an illusion; the libraries of medieval England were not static, still less cumulative, but were often changing, despite the obvious fact that some books remained in the same place for centuries and found the means to survive for centuries more; and it is not possible to think about libraries without thinking about books, because in most contexts throughout the period under review libraries were only one sector of the wider book economy. The perspective has been tilted by the principal two bodies of evidence for libraries, books that carry evidence of institutional provenance and documentary records. This evidence is mostly used in a simple way to discover the provenance of this or that manuscript, to answer the question how many books survive from this or that place, or to investigate how many copies there were of, say, Gregory IX's *Decretales* in medieval England. The list of identifications of the Corpus provides a fairly ready answer to that one – some 300 copies of the *Decretales* attested by documents – but *MLGB* does not, since one must review each entry for contents; apparently it is around 25. Unprovenanced copies are uncounted. I am tempted to drop in the question, how many copies were needed to keep the canon lawyers of England adequately provided? But that question opens up a very large problem about texts and readers and the meeting of needs, which is beyond the scope of this work. Rather it is important to learn to use *MLGB*3 and the body of information presented by volumes of the Corpus to ask more general questions about book provision through libraries of different kinds over five centuries. And having so many of the books themselves, we can enrich the picture that we form from the documents and see how many of the books individually came into libraries from personal ownership and passed out into personal ownership, trade ownership and the ownership of other libraries.

There should be a consistent way of reading the evidence across its breadth and across its *longue durée*. There is always space for closer engagement and serious thinking about one aspect of the evidence, one species of library, or about short periods of activity (or inactivity), but to do that without attempting a bigger picture leaves us with deficient views. The illusory scriptorium of Exeter cathedral in the mid-eleventh century, the prevalent perception of monk-scribes, and the notion of books safely chained in quiet religious houses for centuries all detract from a real understanding of medieval libraries. The subject demands that we try to see it whole.

The end point of the narrative in the 1530s and 1540s is a gloomy one for libraries, but a successful one for books. The big picture must be a mosaic, but it resembles an ancient mosaic, the scene as a whole made up of tesserae that are details, surviving books and entries in booklists; but the evidence is patchy. There are areas where the picture cannot be recovered on English evidence, and there are risks in writing from Continental sources. But it is no good to rely only on the evidence for big Benedictine libraries, which appear to tell such a rich story of Latin learning. For an overview of the medieval libraries, one would be advised to read some of the full catalogues, selected for the type of institution, by size, by period, and a type of library will emerge. One might progress outwards from that to a wider understanding of the matter actually read, then the list of identifications in the Corpus will allow a view of what was widely available, what was not uncommon and what was rare. The close reader will notice rare works, such as St Catherine's *Dialogues*, in Latin translation, appearing only at Syon and in Carthusian libraries but not more widely. The Carthusian writer Denis Ryckel has a similar distribution, and so too the work known as *Donatus deuotionis*. This will not surprise students of late medieval devotional works, but it is good to see it confirmed by the absences represented in such a large index. Negatives themselves can attract attention.

Another negative is vernacular languages. In *MLGB3* 96 per cent of the books entered with an institutional provenance are in Latin, 1 per cent in French, and 3 per cent in English. One has the impression that a considerable number of handwritten books exist in late medieval English (without opening up the material in the public records), but very few of them carry evidence of provenance. They were perhaps all private, but, if so, have they defied the odds in surviving? (Surviving much better than aristocratic books in French from England?) Or were many of them housed at least until the sixteenth century in religious houses that failed to mark their books in an identifiable way? There is a second question to be answered about their survival since the beginning of the sixteenth century, because the libraries that gave safe homes to medieval books in the late sixteenth and seventeenth centuries do not seem to have been much concerned with late-medieval vernacular texts, which therefore survived only in a precarious environment for a very long time. Before conjecturing that they were in the under-attested houses of nuns, I should raise the large question that, across the board, we do not know, in any century, the size of the medieval book economy, and therefore we cannot make any attempt to compute the proportion of that economy represented by libraries.[157] It is a consideration I think we have neglected, and the consequences are various.

Too much focus on monastic books and on libraries as the epicentres of book production in the earlier period has masked openness to recognizing a book trade that did much to make works available and helps us to solve the problem of exemplars. In the later period libraries always draw on the trade but often through individuals, whom we call donors, and they feed the trade with books deaccessioned. This in turn feeds newer libraries, but the intergenerational turnover in books not owned by institutions has always eluded us. We do not know how long a book would last outside a library, and we cannot calibrate how far libraries extended the lifespan of a book. With printed books, Bradshaw's paradox says, If it were rare, it would be common.[158] We know that in later centuries libraries have played a vital role in preserving copies of disregarded works that have become truly rare rather than collectable. The equivalent phenomenon is entirely down to chance with medieval books, since there are no libraries in England that have provided the security to preserve rare works across many hundreds of years. And most medieval texts were in their own day rare and became rarer with time. The evidence we have from medieval libraries is vital to any appreciation of what could be found if a reader wanted to find it, and what was so rare that one could happen across it only by chance. The slender thread is always tempting, but the bigger picture is not something to avoid entirely, however imperfect our attempts may be.

Notes

1. N.R. Ker, *Medieval Libraries of Great Britain*, 1st edn (London, 1941); 2nd edn (London, 1964); Supplement, ed. A.G. Watson (London, 1987); digital 3rd edn (2015), *MLGB3*, available online from the Bodleian Library, Oxford, at http://mlgb3.bodleian.ox.ac.uk.
2. Memoirs of all four men appear in volumes of the *Proceedings of the British Academy*: of Mynors by Michael Winterbottom, vol. 80 (1991), pp. 371–401 (repr. in his *Style and Scholarship: Latin Prose from Gildas to Raffaele Regio. Selected Papers*, ed. R. Gamberini, Florence, 2020, pp. 441–71); of Hunt by Richard Southern, vol. 67 (1981), pp. 371–97; of Cheney by Christopher Brooke, vol. 73 (1987), pp. 425–46; and of Ker by Ian Doyle, vol. 80 (1991), pp. 349–59.
3. Mynors established the text which was then set forth by Mary Rouse and Richard Rouse in their edition of *Registrum Anglie de libris doctorum et auctorum veterum*, CBMLC, 2 (London, 1991); the genesis of the project was given a full treatment in their valuable introduction, pp. xxi–xxix; there is also much of interest in Michael Winterbottom's obituary of Mynors (see n. 2). The Rouses' dating of the *Registrum*, to the second or third decade of the fourteenth century (pp. cxxix–cxxxiv), was on the basis of a perceived relation to the other major production of the Oxford Grey Friars, the *Tabula septem custodiarum*, dated to 1309. John Higgitt (*Scottish Libraries*, CBMLC, 12 (London, 2006), pp. xxxvi–xxxvii), resurrecting an older argument by E.A. Savage, argued that the survey, at least of the Scottish houses, more probably took place before the start of the War of Independence in 1296, since several of the houses whose libraries were reported for the *Registrum*, such as Dunfermline, Kelso and Holyrood, were sacked in the first years of the fourteenth century to presumably catastrophic effect.
4. See further the essays in Cristina Dondi, Dorit Raines and Richard Sharpe (eds), *How the Secularization of Religious Houses Transformed the Libraries of*

Europe, 16th–19th Centuries (Turnhout, forthcoming); in particular Sharpe, 'Dissolution and Dispersal in Sixteenth-Century England: Understanding the Remains'.

5. H. Omont's edition of the Llanthony catalogue (BL MS. Harley 460) appeared in his article 'Anciens catalogues de bibliothèques anglaises', *Centralblatt für Bibliothekswesen* 9 (1892), pp. 201–22, printing four lists: from Burton abbey, an unidentified house now recognized as Bridlington priory, Flaxley abbey, and Llanthony priory (at pp. 207–22).
6. http://mlgb3.bodleian.ox.ac.uk. The project has been under the direction of Prof. Sharpe and Dr James Willoughby and was made possible by grants from the Andrew W. Mellon Foundation and the Neil Ker Memorial Fund. The resource was built by Xiaofeng Yang and Sushila Burgess of Bodleian Digital Library Systems and Services, while Jacob Currie, Peter Kidd, Daniela Mairhofer and David Rundle have all contributed to the work of populating it.
7. It is perhaps worth adding to Professor Sharpe's comment that a further drawback to this decision to exclude registers from *MLGB* is that service books, once Sarum use was general in England, could have been produced anywhere, whereas cartularies and registers were much more likely to have been compiled within an institution and, representing the work of local scribes, can therefore be said to offer more to the work of establishing provenance. But it also bears consideration that Ker knew about the parallel enterprise of G.R.C. Davis to create a Royal Historical Society handlist of cartularies, published as *Medieval Cartularies of Great Britain: A Short Catalogue*, and would not have wished to cut across that effort. The foreword to Davis's first edition of 1958 states that more than a quarter of a century had elapsed 'since medievalists first began to discuss the making of this book'; Neil Ker was thanked for many years of moral and practical support (p. vii).
8. N.R. Ker, 'Medieval Manuscripts from Norwich Cathedral Priory', *Transactions of the Cambridge Bibliographical Society*, Volume 1: *1949–53*, pp. 1–28; repr. in his *Books, Collectors and Libraries: Studies in the Medieval Heritage*, ed. A.G. Watson (London, [1985]), pp. 243–72. See also the discussion in R. Sharpe, J.P. Carley, R.M. Thomson and A.G. Watson, *English Benedictine Libraries: The Shorter Catalogues*, CBMLC, 4 (London, 1996), pp. 289–91.
9. See R. Sharpe, 'Accession, Classification, or Location. Pressmarks in Medieval Libraries', *Scriptorium* 50 (1996), pp. 279–87; also 'Reconstructing the Medieval Library of Bury St Edmunds: The Lost Catalogue of Henry of Kirkstead', in A. Gransden (ed.), *Bury St Edmunds: Medieval Art, Architecture, Archaeology, and Economy*, British Archaeological Association, Conference Transactions 1994 ([Leeds], 1998), pp. 204–18.

10. R.A.B. Mynors, *Catalogue of the Manuscripts of Balliol College, Oxford* (Oxford, 1963), p. 320n.
11. 'Peterhouse, Gonville and Caius, and Pembroke at Cambridge, and Merton, Balliol, New College, Oriel, Lincoln, All Souls, and Magdalen at Oxford have still an appreciable number of their medieval books' (*MLGB2*, p. xv).
12. The first catalogue of incunabula to do a serious job of recording provenance information was the Bodleian's: *A Catalogue of Books Printed in the Fifteenth Century now in the Bodleian Library*, ed. A. Coates, K. Jensen, C. Dondi & others, 6 vols (Oxford, 2005); available online at http://incunables.bodleian.ox.ac.uk. The Material Evidence in Incunabula database (MEI), linked to ISTC, reports copy-specific information from libraries around the world, using every provenance clue to map the sale and movement of books from the beginnings of print to modern times: https://data.cerl.org/mei.
13. The number of books at Durham aggregates catalogues of the books in the *spendement* in 1392 and in the cloister in 1395, together representing the principal accumulations of books in the priory; these lists are found in MS. B. IV. 46 in the Cathedral Library; an edition gathered by the late Alan Piper is forthcoming (see further below, n. 27). The Canterbury list referred to is the extensive catalogue drawn up in the time of Prior Henry of Eastry, in what is now BL MS. Cotton Galba E. IV; a new edition is forthcoming by James Willoughby.
14. For the early-modern evidence, see the catalogue of the Worcester manuscripts drawn up by Patrick Young (1584–1652), *Catalogus librorum manuscriptorum bibliothecae Wigorniensis: Made in 1622–1623*, ed. N.R. Ker and I. Atkins (Cambridge, 1944). See also Rodney M. Thomson, *A Descriptive Catalogue of the Medieval Manuscripts in Worcester Cathedral Library* (Cambridge, 2001).
15. C.F.R. de Hamel, 'The Dispersal of the Library of Christ Church, Canterbury, from the Fourteenth to the Sixteenth Century', in J.P. Carley and C.G.C. Tite (eds), *Books and Collectors 1200–1700: Essays presented to Andrew Watson* (London, 1997), pp. 263–79; A.G. Watson, 'John Twyne of Canterbury (d. 1581) as a Collector of Medieval Manuscripts: A Preliminary Investigation', *The Library*, 6th series, 8 (1986), pp. 133–51.
16. N.R. Ker, 'The Migration of Manuscripts from the English Medieval Libraries', *The Library*, 4th series, 23 (1942), pp. 1–11, being his lecture read before the Bibliographical Society the previous year; repr. in his *Books, Collectors and Libraries*, pp. 459–70.
17. See James Willoughby, 'John Erghome and the Library of the Austin Friars of York', in C. Saunders and R. Lawrie (eds), *Middle English Manuscripts and Their Legacies: A Volume in Honour of Ian Doyle* (Leiden, 2022), pp. 96–117, arguing that the catalogue of the library at the York Austins was

inaugurated by John Erghome himself. Professor Sharpe's preference for 'Argam' for the figure who called himself 'Erghome' or 'Ergome' acknowledges the modern spelling of the village of Argam in Yorkshire from which the surname derived.

18. Llanthony books seem to have remained in the area after the dissolution, in the hands of the last prior, Richard Hart, who was given rights of residence on the priory's former property at Brockworth, near Gloucester. At his death in 1545 he left all his 'bookes of latyn' to one Thomas Morgan, perhaps a former confrère. His executor, his sister's husband, was Thomas Theyer of Brockworth, through whose grandson, John Theyer, so many Llanthony books passed to the royal library *c.*1678. Many others are in Lambeth Palace Library through Archbishop Bancroft's benefaction. Andrew Watson, in his discussion of the descent of the Llanthony manuscripts (T. Webber and A.G. Watson (eds), *The Libraries of the Augustinian Canons*, CBMLC, 6 (London, 1998), p. 35), described their acquisition by Archbishop Bancroft as 'a mystery which seems unlikely ever to be solved'. M.R. James had, however, argued quite plausibly that Bancroft had acquired a portion of the collection at an earlier date, from the elder Theyer, since the manuscripts are visible in lists of Lambeth books received by the University of Cambridge during the Protectorate (*The Manuscripts in the Library at Lambeth Palace*, Cambridge Antiquarian Society, Octavo Publications, 33 (1900), pp. 1–6, at p. 6).
19. Simon Horobin and Aditi Nafde, 'Stephan Batman and the Making of the Parker Library', *Transactions of the Cambridge Bibliographical Society* 15 (2015), pp. 561–81. For a census of Batman's books, see M.B. Parkes, 'Stephan Batman's Manuscripts', in Masahiko Kanno and others (eds), *Medieval Heritage: Essays in Honour of Tadahiro Ikegami* (Tokyo, 1997), pp. 125–56; repr. with addenda in P.R. Robinson and Rivkah Zim (eds), *Pages from the Past: Medieval Writing Skills and Manuscript Books* (Farnham, 2012); also A.S.G. Edwards and Simon Horobin, 'Further Books Annotated by Stephen Batman', *The Library*, 7th series, 11 (2010), pp. 227–31; and A.B. Kraebel, 'A Further Book Annotated by Stephan Batman, with New Material for His Biography', *The Library*, 7th series, 16 (2015), pp. 458–66.
20. J.B.L. Tolhurst, *The Ordinale and Customary of the Benedictine Nuns of Barking Abbey: University College, Oxford, MS. 169*, 2 vols, Henry Bradshaw Society, 65–6 (London, 1927–8), vol. 1, pp. 67–8. For the custumals of Westminster and St Augustine's, see *Customary of the Benedictine Monasteries of St Augustine, Canterbury, and St Peter, Westminster*, ed. E.M. Thompson, 2 vols, Henry Bradshaw Society, 23, 28 (London, 1902–4).
21. For a recent attempt to use *MLGB3* to estimate numbers of lost books, see Eltjo Buringh, 'Loss Rates of Medieval English and Scottish Books',

forthcoming; also his 'The Role of Medieval Cities in Book Production: Quantitative Analyses', in Marco Mostert and Anna Adamska (eds), *Uses of the Written Word in Medieval Towns: Medieval Urban Literacy II* (Turnhout, 2014), pp. 119–77.

22. See further Alan Coates, *English Medieval Books: The Reading Abbey Collections from Foundation to Dispersal* (Oxford, 1999), p. 53; also Sharpe, *English Benedictine Libraries*, p. 419.
23. Richard Sharpe, 'The Medieval Librarian', in *A History of Libraries in Britain and Ireland*, Volume 1: *From the Beginnings to 1640*, ed. E.S. Leedham-Green and M.T.J. Webber (Cambridge, 2006), pp. 218–41.
24. For Henry of Kirkestede, see Rouse and Rouse, *Registrum Anglie*; and their *Henry of Kirkestede, Catalogus de libris autenticis et apocrifis*, CBMLC, 11 (London, 2004); also Sharpe, 'Reconstructing the Medieval Library of Bury St Edmunds'; and see further below.
25. Equally, there may be sorrow when a book once recognized as belonging to a particular house comes to be rejected. While some of these identifications were built on the back of little more than an intangible suggestion by M.R. James, sometimes the decision is of a finer grain which it would benefit the user to know. But the digital version of *MLGB* has proved unable to handle rejects as it cannot isolate them from the positive identifications. It is hoped that this aspect of the representation will be improved in a future release, perhaps by use of flat files.
26. For Monk Bretton, see Joseph Hunter, *South Yorkshire* (London, 1828–31; repr. Wakefield, 1974), vol. 2, pp. 274–6, and again in his *English Monastic Libraries* (London, 1831), pp. 1–7; the catalogue has been printed most recently in Sharpe, *English Benedictine Libraries*, pp. 266–87 (B55). For Hinton, see Hunter, *English Monastic Libraries*, pp. 16–19, printing an English précis of an indenture of 1343 then belonging to Thomas Phillipps and since untraced; this précis was reprinted with discussion by A.I. Doyle, *The Libraries of the Carthusians*, CBMLC, 9 (London, 2001), pp. 611–14 (C1).
27. [B. Botfield], *Catalogi veteres ecclesiae cathedralis Dunelmensis*, Surtees Society, 1 (1838). (Botfield also reprinted, p. xxxviii, the Hinton list mentioned in the preceding note.) Botfield's work for Durham will be finally superseded by the late Alan Piper's volume on Durham cathedral priory and its cells, forthcoming in the Corpus of British Medieval Library Catalogues. See further Piper's 'The Libraries of the Monks of Durham', in M.B. Parkes and A.G. Watson (eds), *Medieval Scribes, Manuscripts and Libraries: Essays presented to N.R. Ker* (London, 1978), pp. 213–49; also A.I. Doyle, 'The Printed Books of the Last Monks of Durham', *The Library*, 7th series, 10 (1988), pp. 203–19.
28. John Nichols, *The History and Antiquities of the County of Leicester*, 8 pts in 4 vols (London, for the author, 1795–1815), vol. 1, pt 2, Appendix xvii, pp.

101–8; R. Sharpe, 'Henry Ellis, Richard Gough's Protégé', *Bodleian Library Record* 22 (2009), pp. 191–211, at p. 198.

29. See below, p. 123. A contemporary of James's in Cambridge, Mary Bateson (1865–1906), fellow of Newnham College, was a historian of extraordinary reach as well as a prominent suffragist.
30. Considerations about how references to works read in the Middle Ages can and should be stabilized, with some insightful worked examples, form the subject of Richard Sharpe's *Titulus. Identifying Medieval Latin Texts: An Evidence-Based Approach* (Turnhout, 2003).
31. In fact, volumes of the Corpus still to be published when Professor Sharpe was writing do include such lists. There is an inventory of 1421 of the chancery at Durham (Durham Cathedral Muniments, Reg. II, fol. 156v), an inventory of registers of 1447 from St Paul's Cathedral (London Metropolitan Archives, former Guildhall Library MSS 25511A and 25511), and another of 1499 of the muniments of Lincoln cathedral (Lincoln, Lincolnshire Archives, Lincoln Dean and Chapter Archive, Chapter Act Book 1479–1496, A/3/1, fol. 158r). It remains the case that such lists are not common.
32. Linked inventories surviving from 1245, 1255 and 1295 describe books by appearance, the opening and closing texts inside, sometimes a mention of the script if it is unusual (not merely 'de bona littera' but also 'de scotica littera' and 'anglice littere') and description of the illumination; James M.W. Willoughby and Nigel Ramsay (eds), *The Libraries of the Secular Cathedrals*, CBMLC, 17 (London, 2023), SC87–89. The fullest listing of the chapter's books is an inventory of 1458 reporting 161 books on the desks of the new library (ibid., SC104). This had been set up, remarkably, as a library of common resort, open at set hours of the day and staffed by two chaplain-librarians. The regulations governing this library were clearly inspired by those of the common library at Guildhall in the city, established in 1422 and celebrated now as England's first 'public' library. The impetus for the foundation of this and several other closely related libraries of common resort, valued as supports for sound clerical instruction, is discussed by James Willoughby, 'Common Libraries in Fifteenth-Century England: An Episcopal Benefaction', in V.A. Gillespie and K. Ghosh (eds), *After Arundel: Religious Writing in Fifteenth-Century England* (Turnhout, 2011), pp. 209–22. The inspiration for this movement is traced to the milieu at Oriel College, Oxford, in the 1420s, where key figures were fellows together. One more of that number, Thomas Graunt, who was subsequently elected a canon of St Paul's in 1452, was the probable instigator of the plan for the common library at St Paul's.
33. The list of volumes in the Corpus are defined in the Abbreviations list above.
34. Rouse and Rouse, *Registrum Anglie*; and their *Henry of Kirkestede*.

35. Rouse and Rouse, *Henry of Kirkestede*, pp. xciv–xcv. Some may have been lost already in Jerome's time, since, as he acknowledged in his prologue, he copied a number of titles from Eusebius: *De viris illustribus*, ed. Aldo Ceresa-Gastaldo (Florence, 1988); for a recent discussion, see Irene SanPietro, 'The Making of a Christian Intellectual Tradition in Jerome's *De viris illustribus*', *Memoirs of the American Academy in Rome* 62 (2017), pp. 231–60.
36. On the Italian lists, anonymous and undated but surviving in a copy partially in the hand of Cardinal Marcello Cervini, the future Pope Marcellus II, see James Willoughby, 'Cardinal Marcello Cervini (1501–1555) and English Libraries', in James Willoughby and Jeremy Catto (eds), *Books and Bookmen in Early Modern Britain: Essays Presented to James P. Carley* (Toronto, 2018), pp. 119–49, the lists printed at pp. 135–49; also Willoughby, 'Italian Evidence for Duke Humfrey's Library before its Dispersal', *Bodleian Library Record* 31 (2018), pp. 20–30. The tour of Lincolnshire can be dated to the summer of 1528 on the grounds that the agents declared themselves unable to enter certain religious houses because of an outbreak of the sweating sickness; this epidemic occurred in the summer of 1528 and Lincolnshire was particularly hard hit; see J.P. Carley, *John Leland, De viris illustribus: On Famous Men* (Toronto and Oxford, 2010), p. lxii n. 198. These Lincolnshire lists were printed by J.R. Liddell, '"Leland's" Lists of Manuscripts in Lincolnshire Monasteries', *English Historical Review* 54 (1939), pp. 88–95; for context, see Carley, *Libraries of Henry VIII*, pp. xxxiii–xxxv, and for some observations on its compilation, see James M.W. Willoughby, *The Libraries of Collegiate Churches*, CBMLC, 15 (London, 2013), pp. 533–5. The entries in both lists have been separately excerpted and printed under their institutional headings in respective volumes of the Corpus of British Medieval Library Catalogues.
37. Leland's antiquarian researches have been famous since his own day. The notes which he made during his various bibliographical tours of the country are preserved in quarto notebooks in the Bodleian, principally MS. Top. gen. c. 3: these, as with the lists mentioned in the previous note, have been separately printed under their institutional headings in respective volumes of the Corpus of British Medieval Library Catalogues. Leland's work and the chronology of the tours have been finally elucidated by Carley, *John Leland, De viris illustribus*, esp. pp. li–c.
38. For further examination of a typology of the evidence, see Richard Sharpe, 'Library Catalogues and Indexes', in *The Cambridge History of the Book in Britain*, Volume 2: *1100–1400*, ed. Nigel J. Morgan and Rodney M. Thomson (Cambridge, 2008), pp. 197–218.
39. The catalogue, described internally as a *matricularium librarie*, is discussed by Karsten Friis-Jensen and James M.W. Willoughby, *Peterborough Abbey*, CBMLC, 8 (London, 2001), pp. xxx–xxxi, 49–54.

40. For orientation, see James M.W. Willoughby, 'The *Secundo Folio* and its Uses, Medieval and Modern', *The Library*, 7th series, 12 (2011), pp. 237–58.
41. Mention might also be made in this connection of seventeen books given to the Domus Dei at Ewelme (Oxon) by Alice Chaucer, duchess of Suffolk, in 1466; see N.L. Ramsay and James M.W. Willoughby, *Hospitals, Towns, and the Professions* (eds), CBMLC, 14 (London, 2009), pp. 44–9 (SH14). The material, largely liturgical and devotional, also included Christine de Pisan and a copy of *Le Jugement dou Roy de Behaingne* of Guillaume de Machaut, a work to which Alice's grandfather, Geoffrey Chaucer, happened to owe a literary debt, as seen especially in his *Book of the Duchess*. Was Alice passing on to her hospital a book from her grandfather's collection? Other examples are the clutch of romances left to Evesham abbey by Prior Nicholas of Hereford (d. 1392) (B30. 69–74) and others reported in the *Matricularium* of Peterborough abbey (BP21. 203, 331, 338).
42. The chapter library remained remarkably stable across time, such that about a third of the books given to the church by Bishop Leofric around 1072 (SC19) may be identified today among those given to Thomas Bodley by the dean and chapter in 1602, remaining in the Bodleian Library. More than 150 books reported in the catalogue of 1327 (SC20) – more than half its number – are visible in the inventory of 1506.
43. See Piper, 'Libraries of the Monks of Durham', and references above at nn. 13, 27.
44. Rouse and Rouse, *Kirkestede*, pp. xliii–li; Sharpe, 'Reconstructing the Medieval Library of Bury St Edmunds'. The Rouses conclude that 'it would be imprudent to say whether the total was closer to 1,500 or 2,000; but it is obvious that Bury's collection of books was very large relative to those of other English abbeys' (p. li).
45. Willoughby, 'The *Secundo Folio* and its Uses', pp. 237–41.
46. Rouse and Rouse, *Registrum*, pp. l–lv. The Crowland list is now Berlin, Stiftung Preussischer Kulturbesitz, MS. Hamilton 30, fol. 123r.
47. M.R. James, *The Ancient Libraries of Canterbury and Dover: The Catalogues of the Libraries of Christ Church Priory and St Augustine's Abbey at Canterbury, and of St Martin's Priory at Dover* (Cambridge, 1903); James, 'Lists of Manuscripts Formerly in Peterborough Abbey Library', *Trans. Bibliographical Society*, Supplement 5 (1926); James, 'Catalogue of the Library of Leicester Abbey', *Transactions of the Leicestershire Archaeological Society* 19 (1936–7), pp. 118–61, 378–440, and 21 (1939–41), pp. 1–88. He also printed another very interesting specimen: 'Catalogue of the Library of the Augustinian Friars at York'. Also Mary Bateson, *Catalogue of the Library of Syon Monastery Isleworth* (Cambridge, 1898).

48. B.C. Barker-Benfield, *St Augustine's Abbey, Canterbury*, CBMLC, 13, 3 vols (London, 2008), esp. pp. 3–7.
49. For the early library at Durham, see R.A.B. Mynors, *Durham Cathedral Manuscripts to the End of the Twelfth Century* (Oxford, 1939); and Michael Gullick, 'The Scribe of the Carilef Bible: A New Look at Some Late-Eleventh-Century Durham Cathedral Manuscripts', in Linda L. Brownrigg (ed.), *Medieval Book Production: Assessing the Evidence. Proceedings of the Second Conference of the Seminar in the History of the Book to 1500, Oxford, July 1988* (Los Altos Hills CA, 1990), pp. 61–83.
50. Geoffrey of Burton, *Life and Miracles of St Modwenna*, ed. Robert Bartlett (Oxford, 2002).
51. Besides these two copies, there is a bifolium used to bind a booklet of acts passed by a single session of Parliament in the time of Edward VI, now BL MS. Add. 63642. Library catalogues attest three copies for Burton abbey in the late twelfth century (B11. 2b, 32), one at Ramsey abbey in the fourteenth century (B68. 374), while copies were seen by Leland with the Cistercians of Revesby in Lincolnshire (Z17. 1) and by Bale at Glastonbury (B45. 38a); the nuns of Romsey had an abbreviation in the fourteenth century, in a collection of abbreviated saints' lives most likely edited in-house. See further Geoffrey of Burton, *Life and Miracles of St Modwenna*, ed. Bartlett, pp. xl–xliii.
52. The inventory of Exeter cathedral, drawn up in 1327, merits inclusion alongside these other two. In its abbreviated references it resembles the Ramsey lists; the potential, however, for cross-matching with the cathedral's many surviving books permits an excellent view of the foundation collection ossified in the first part of the record, before, in the latter part, books were arranged under donor headings, beginning with William Warelwast, bishop from 1107 to 1137; see Willoughby and Ramsay, *Secular Cathedrals*, SC20.
53. A valuable introduction to the subject is provided by Joan Greatrex, *The English Benedictine Cathedral Priories: Rule and Practice* (Oxford, 2011), pp. 126–59. Also Henry Wansbrough and Anthony Marett-Crosby (eds), *Benedictines in Oxford* (London, 1997).
54. N.R. Ker, *English Manuscripts in the Century after the Norman Conquest: The Lyell Lectures 1952–3* (Oxford, 1960).
55. T. Webber, 'Script and Manuscript Production at Christ Church, Canterbury, after the Norman Conquest', in Richard Eales and Richard Sharpe (eds), *Canterbury and the Norman Conquest: Churches, Saints, and Scholars 1066–1109* (London, 1995), pp. 145–58; also Michael Gullick, 'The Scribal Work of Eadmer of Canterbury to 1109', *Archaeologia Cantiana* 118 (1998), pp. 173–89.

56. Samu Niskanen (ed.), *Epistolae Anselmi Cantuariensis Archiepiscopi: Letters of Anselm, Archbishop of Canterbury*, Volume I: *The Bec Letters* (Oxford, 2019) (vol. 2 forthcoming); for example, epp. 10, 19, 21, 31–2, 35, 51, 57, 61–4, 99, 127, 130, 132.
57. T. Webber, *Scribes and Scholars at Salisbury Cathedral, c.1075–c.1125* (Oxford, 1992).
58. A full digital surrogate of the manuscript, together with a detailed palaeographical and codicological description, is available at www.exondomesday.ac.uk, being *Exon: The Domesday Survey of South-West England*, ed. P.A. Stokes, Studies in Domesday, gen. ed. J.C. Crick (London, 2018); see also F.L. Álvarez López and J.C. Crick, 'Decision-Making and Work Flow in the Making of Exon Domesday', in B.A. Shailor and C. Dutschke (eds), *Scribes and the Presentation of Texts (from Antiquity to c.1550): Proceedings of the 20th Colloquium of the Comité international de paléographie latine* (Turnhout, 2021), pp. 155–75.
59. T.D. Hardy, *Descriptive Catalogue of Materials Relating to the History of Great Britain and Ireland to the End of the Reign of Henry VII*, Rolls Series 26, 4 pts in 3 vols (London, 1862–71), vol. 3, pp. xi–xv.
60. E. Martène, *De antiquis Ecclesiae ritibus libri quatuor*, 2nd edn, 3 vols (Milan, 1736–7), vol. 3, Appendix, cols 733–6.
61. J.W. Clark, *The Observances in Use at the Augustinian Priory of S. Giles and S. Andrew at Barnwell, Cambridgeshire* (Cambridge, 1897), pp. xxxix–xlvii.
62. *Gesta abbatum monasterii Sancti Albani*, ed. H.T. Riley, Rolls Series 28, 3 vols (London, 1867–9), vol. 1, pp. 57–8. While the emphasis is on the assignment of income to pay for the hire of scribes, this paragraph ends by referring 'continuo in ipso quod construxit scriptorio libros preelectos scribi fecit'.
63. Ibid., pp. 183–4, 192.
64. Brian Golding, *Gilbert of Sempringham and the Gilbertine Order c.1130–c.1300* (Oxford, 1995), pp. 181–2, 184; R. Graham, *S. Gilbert of Sempringham and the Gilbertines: A History of the Only English Monastic Order* (London, 1901), p. 61.
65. See *Gesta abbatum*, vol. 3, p. 281: 'Per idem tempus sederunt ministri dicti Episcopi [*sc.* William Courtenay, archbishop of Canterbury 1381–96] in ecclesia de Hatfeld, inter cetera inquirentes quo titulo Scriptorarius Sancti Albani tenet duas partes decimarum in eadem parochia de toto dominio Nicolai filii Simonis; vocaveruntque dictum Scripturarium ad comparendum et docendum quo jure tenet decimas supradictas. Sed Scripturarius non comparuit, eoque exemptus fuit. Quamobrem onerata duodena de patria, cognoverunt quod a tempore quo non extat memoria gavisus fuit pacifice decimis memoratis' (in margin: 'Pro officio Cantoris vel Scriptorarii'); ibid., pp. 392–3 (this latter coming not from BL MS. Cotton Claudius E. IV but from the 'continuation' in Cambridge, Corpus

Christi College, MS. 7): 'Testantur que dico [that is, the good uses to which abbot Thomas de la Mare expended money] domus Scriptorie, sumptibus ipsius Abbatis, et industria Domini Thome de Walsingham, tunc Cantoris et Scriptorarii, a fundamentis constructa; libri etiam per ipsum et suos conscripti, empti, et reparati, et librarie Conventus et Studii sui deputati'.

66. While the view that Norman tastes brought old libraries in England into a Continental mainstream had long been axiomatic, it was first explored in detail by Ker, *English Manuscripts in the Century After the Norman Conquest*; see also Rodney M. Thomson, *Books and Learning in Twelfth-Century England: The Ending of 'alter orbis'. The Lyell Lectures 2000–2001* (Walkern, 2006); T. Webber, 'Monastic and Cathedral Book Collections in the Late Eleventh and Twelfth Centuries', in *Cambridge History of Libraries in Britain and Ireland*, vol. 1, ed. Leedham-Green and Webber, pp. 109–25. Richard Gameson, 'The Circulation of Books Between England and the Continent, *c.*871–*c.*1100', in *The Cambridge History of the Book in Britain*, Volume 1: *c.400–1100*, ed. R. Gameson (Cambridge, 2011), pp. 344–72, at pp. 365–8; also James Willoughby, 'The Transmission and Circulation of Classical Literature: Libraries and Florilegia', in *The Oxford History of Classical Reception in English Literature*, Volume 1: *800–1558*, ed. R. Copeland (Oxford, 2016), pp. 98–101.
67. See Nigel Ramsay, 'Law', in *Cambridge History of the Book in Britain*, vol. 2, ed. Morgan and Thomson, pp. 250–90.
68. *Gesta abbatum*, ed. Riley, vol. 1, p. 105, names the Italian Wodo, but David Smith, *English Episcopal Acta 1, Lincoln, 1067–1185* (London, 1980), p. xli, makes him Wido.
69. *Gesta abbatum*, ed. Riley, vol. 1, p. 105.
70. For example, the custumal of St Augustine's abbey, Canterbury: 'libri quos habet de librario, et alii libri de acquisicione sua, omnia ista liberentur precentori; et ipse scribere faciet nomen fratris in quolibet libro de sua acquisicione, antequam portentur in librarium'; *Customary of St Augustine, Canterbury, and St Peter, Westminster*, ed. Thompson, vol. 1, p. 362. The customs of Peterborough abbey governing the Lenten distribution of reading books among the brethren and the solemn commemoration of donors to the library on the first Monday and Tuesday in Lent are suggestive of another context in which the identity of a book's donor it would have been valuable to know; Friis-Jensen and Willoughby, *Peterborough Abbey*, pp. xxviii–xxix, xliii–xlvi.
71. David M. Smith and Vera C.M. London, *The Heads of Religious Houses, England and Wales*, Volume II: *1216–1377* (Cambridge, 2001), p. 61.
72. Ibid., p. 128, citing only the evidence of the Ramsey abbey catalogue.

73. *OED*, 2nd edn (1989), *s.v.* stationer[1], citing *Memoranda Roll 45 & 46 Hen. III*, m. 9b.
74. University statutes banned the 'Four Stationers' from accessing pledged items without supervision and required an oath of office, sworn annually, binding a stationer to make accurate appraisals; *Statuta antiqua universitatis Oxoniensis*, ed. Strickland Gibson (Oxford, 1931), pp. 159–63, 183–7. See further Parkes, 'Provision of Books', pp. 451–2, 465–6, and his 'Thomas Hunt and the Oxford Book-Business in the Late Fifteenth Century', *The Library*, 7th series, 17 (2016), pp. 28–39; also J. Adams, 'Thomas Hunt's Monograms', *The Library*, 7th series, 22 (2021), pp. 376–82.
75. From 1350: 'caucio per publicum stacionarium fideliter estimetur et subhastetur et plus offerenti detur'; *Statuta antiqua Oxoniensis*, ed. Gibson, p. 78.
76. A.N.L. Munby, 'Notes on King's College Library in the Fifteenth Century', *Transactions of the Cambridge Bibliographical Society*, vol. 1 (1949–53), pp. 280–86, at pp. 282–3, repr. in his *Essays and Papers* (London, 1977), pp. 27–36, at pp. 28–31; Willoughby, *Collegiate Churches*, pp. 123–4. The original letter is letter is PRO, Chancery Warrants for the Great Seal, C 81/1444/2, endorsed 21 March 1447.
77. C.P. Christianson, *A Directory of London Stationers and Book Artisans, 1300–1500* (New York, 1990), pp. 145–8.
78. John Leland (*De viris illustribus*, ed. J.P. Carley, *John Leland, De viris illustribus. On Famous Men* (Toronto and Oxford, 2010), p. 736) says that Netter gave to the library a great number of books, 'written in Roman majuscule script', but does not distinguish which in his list of sixty-one titles he saw at the house derived from this benefaction. Three surviving books carry inscriptions that they were given to the London Carmel by him: Cambridge, St John's College, MS. I. 15 (computus); Oxford, Bodleian Library, MS. Bodl. 730 (Cassian's *Collationes*); and Oxford, Trinity College, MS. 58 (a glossed psalter). For Netter's life and career, see the article by Anne Hudson in *ODNB*.
79. John Bale, *Scriptorum illustrium Maioris Brytanniae catalogus*, 2nd edn, 2 pts (Basel: Apud Ioannem Oporinum, 1557–9), pt 1, p. 504.
80. For a catalogue raisonné of the survivors from the library at Buildwas abbey, see Jennifer M. Sheppard, *The Buildwas Books: Book Production, Acquisition and Use at an English Cistercian Monastery, 1165–c. 1400*, Oxford Bibliographical Society Publications, 3rd series, 2 (Oxford, 1997).
81. On Gascoigne, see R.M. Ball, *Thomas Gascoigne, Libraries and Scholarship*, Cambridge Bibliographical Society Monographs, 14 (Cambridge, 2006).
82. David Knowles, C.N.L. Brooke and Vera C.M. London, *The Heads of Religious Houses, England and Wales*, Volume 1: *940–1216* (Cambridge, 2001),

p. 77; R. Sharpe, *A Handlist of the Latin Writers of Great Britain and Ireland before 1540* (Turnhout, 1997), p. 365.

83. One from the priory of St Peter at Eye in Suffolk, a cell of Bernay, has the inscription, after the *ex libris*, 'Omnes eum vid[entes?] minime venalem esse'; it is now Oxford, Magdalen College, MS. lat. 170, a copy of Geoffrey of Monmouth from the late twelfth or early thirteenth century. Sale was a hazard for books, and this inscription is a reminder that books regarded as having no textual value might be sold instead for their materials, discussed further in Chapter 6 below.
84. Willoughby, *Collegiate Churches*, p. 868.
85. Oxford, Bodleian Library, MS. Bodl. 543 is given a double provenance, Ramsey and Worcester, because it contains a deed of agreement between the two and Ker could not determine in which location this copy was kept.
86. In fact, although Bishop Grandisson was an opulent patron to his cathedral and very interested in its chapter library, he owned many more books than he presented to the chapter. His books were examined in detail by M.W. Steele, 'A Study of the Books Owned or Used by John Grandisson, Bishop of Exeter', D.Phil. thesis (University of Oxford, 1994); the matter is revisited by Willoughby and Ramsay, *Secular Cathedrals*. Convenient lists of Grandisson's identified books were printed by A.B. Emden, *A Biographical Register of the University of Oxford to A.D. 1500*, 3 vols (Oxford, 1957–59), pp. 800–801: those that passed to Exeter, those that belonged to him, and those containing notes in his own hand.
87. Willoughby, *Collegiate Churches*, p. 868. Some of these ex-monastic books were given by King Edward IV: Oxford, Bodleian Library, MSS. Bodl. 192 and 729 (*SC* 2099, 2706); both have labels on the lower boards with the inscription 'Ex dono illustrissimi regis Edwardi iiij^ti'. Bodley 192 is a mid-twelfth-century copy of Gregory's *Homiliae super euangeliis* written by cooperating scribes at Rouen, and Bodley 729 is a copy of Bede on Luke and Mark of the same date, with an earlier provenance of the Augustinian abbey at Missenden. Willoughby (*Collegiate Churches*, pp. 868–9) suggests that the king had simply settled the canons' bills with a stationer, or that his agent had arranged to buy from available stock, and he puts the date of donation around 1480, when the new library room was being built.
88. See Anne Hudson's article on Netter in *ODNB*.
89. Gillespie, *Syon Abbey*, pp. xlv, lxv. The library and literacy of the sisters of Syon have received considerable attention: see principally C.F.R. de Hamel, *Syon Abbey: The Library of the Bridgettine Nuns and their Peregrinations after the Reformation*, Roxburghe Club (London, 1991); Ann Hutchison, '"To yowr gostly comforte and proffite": Devotional Reading for the Nuns of Syon Abbey', in V. Blanton, V. O'Mara and P. Stoop (eds), *Nuns' Literacies*

in Medieval Europe: The Antwerp Dialogue, Medieval Women: Texts and Contexts, 28 (Turnhout, 2017), pp. 61–82; Virginia R. Bainbridge, 'Syon Abbey: Women and Learning *c.*1415–1600', in E.A. Jones and A. Walsham (eds), *Syon Abbey and its Books: Reading, Writing and Religion, c.1400–1700* (Woodbridge, 2010), pp. 82–103.

90. Generally, Reed was buying rather than commissioning books: many are marked *emptus* in inscriptions that commemorate his patron, Nicholas of Sandwich. Further discussion in Rodney M. Thomson, 'William Reed, Bishop of Chichester (d. 1385) – Bibliophile?', in G.H. Brown and L.E. Voigts (eds), *The Study of Medieval Manuscripts of England: Festschrift in Honor of Richard W. Pfaff* (Tempe AZ, 2010), pp. 281–93.
91. Cambridge, Pembroke College, MS. 7, containing the note by Robert Grosseteste at fol. 1v: 'Memoriale magistri Roberti Grossetes' pro Exameron Basilii'. See further B. Smalley, 'A Collection of Paris Lectures of the Later Twelfth Century in the MS. Pembroke College, Cambridge 7', *Cambridge Historical Journal* 6 (1938), pp. 103–13, at pp. 103–4. Grosseteste was a Suffolk man by birth and seems to have maintained a connection with the monks at Bury St Edmunds, sending them around 1238 his long précis of a Greek work on the monastic life (ep. 57; *Roberti Grosseteste Episcopi quondam Lincolniensis epistolae*, ed. H.R. Luard, Rolls Series, 25 (1861), pp. 173–8; translated by F.A.C. Mantello, *The Letters of Robert Grosseteste, Bishop of Lincoln* (Toronto, 2010), pp. 200–204).
92. The book was described with reference to the title 'Iohannes Chrysostomus de laude apostoli' and two other works; it appears as entry 214 in the Eastry catalogue. It was presumably back in place when reported at Christ Church in *Registrum Anglie* a generation earlier (one of eight copies at R9. 25). The transaction is documented by a letter of Prior Nicholas to the prior of Anglesey, where the books of the borrower had gone after his death; it survives among documents from there now in the National Archives, PRO, E40/14474; *The Letters and Charters of Cardinal Guala Bicchieri, 1216–1218*, ed. N.C. Vincent, Canterbury & York Society, 83 (Woodbridge, 1996), no. 156. The letter was first printed by Joseph Burtt, 'Notes Upon Ancient Libraries', *Notes & Queries* 1 (1849), pp. 21–3.
93. Only the response survives, identified as coming from Geoffrey Lambourn, abbot of Eynsham 1351–88, and datable 1363 × 1366, by W.A. Pantin, *Documents Illustrating the Activities of the General and Provincial Chapters of the English Black Monks, 1215–1540*, Camden Society, 3rd series, 45, 47, 54 (London, 1931–37), vol. 3, pp. 34–51; the relevant article (§47) was excerpted in Sharpe, *English Benedictine Libraries*, pp. 153–4 (B33). Nine books and several borrowers are mentioned, some of the loans demanded by bishops.
94. Printed from a chapter register by J.B. Sheppard, *Literae Cantuarienses: The*

Letter Books of the Monastery of Christ Church, Canterbury, Rolls Series, 85 (London, 1887–89), vol. 2, pp. 146–52 (no. 618); excerpted by James, *Ancient Libraries*, pp. 146–9, and again by Willoughby, *Christ Church*.

95. Parkes, 'Provision of Books', pp. 449–52; Greatrex, *English Benedictine Cathedral Priories*, p. 131.
96. Richard Gameson, *The Medieval Manuscripts of Trinity College, Oxford: A Descriptive Catalogue*, Oxford Bibliographical Society Publications, Special Series, Manuscript Catalogues, 3 (Oxford, 2018), p. 331, acknowledging Rewley but preferring Kirkstead.
97. See Ball, *Thomas Gascoigne, Libraries, and Scholarship*.
98. On his gifts to Merton, see Thomson, *Oxford*, pp. 958–62 (UO56); for Tattershall, see Willoughby, *Collegiate Churches*, pp. 524–5, 537–8.
99. Rodney M. Thomson, *A Descriptive Catalogue of the Medieval Manuscripts of Merton College, Oxford* (Cambridge, 2009), p. 135.
100. See further below, p. 105.
101. The booklist has been much discussed and printed, most pertinently by Michael Lapidge, 'Surviving Book-Lists from Anglo-Saxon England', in M. Lapidge and H. Gneuss (eds), *Learning and Literature in Anglo-Saxon England: Studies Presented to Peter Clemoes on the Occasion of his Sixty-Fifth Birthday* (Cambridge, 1985), pp. 33–89; repr. in M.P. Richards (ed.), *Anglo-Saxon Manuscripts: Basic Readings* (New York and London, 1994), pp. 87–169. See also the discussion by Simon Keynes, 'King Athelstan's Books', in Lapidge and H. Gneuss (eds), *Learning and Literature in Anglo-Saxon England*, pp. 143–201, esp. pp. 172–3. Alan Piper's view that the document's credibility 'is open to serious question' is given full treatment in his forthcoming volume on Durham Cathedral for the Corpus of British Medieval Library Catalogues.
102. George Hickes and Humfrey Wanley, *Antiquae literaturae septentrionalis libri duo*, 2 vols (Oxford: E Theatro Sheldoniano, 1705), vol. 2, p. 238.
103. Most recently to accompany Tessa Webber's discussion in P. Binski and S. Panayotova (eds), *The Cambridge Illuminations: Ten Centuries of Book Production in the Medieval West* (London, 2005), no. 111.
104. Michael Lapidge, *The Anglo-Saxon Library* (Oxford, 2006), now supported by Helmut Gneuss and Michael Lapidge, *Anglo-Saxon Manuscripts: A Bibliographical Handlist of Manuscripts and Manuscript Fragments Written or Owned in England up to 1100* (Toronto, 2014). For the attribution to Acca, see Lapidge, 'Acca of Hexham and the Origin of the *Old English Martyrology*', *Analecta Bollandiana* 123 (2005), pp. 29–78.
105. Notes which accompany this booklist include a pedigree of the counts of Flanders to Baldwin VII, so might be presumed to date from the time when he was count, between 1111 and 1119. James Willoughby has proposed

that the booklist is a record of what had survived a devastating fire at the monastery in 1116; Friis-Jensen and Willoughby, *Peterborough Abbey*, p. 7.

106. The list has been frequently printed and discussed from the time of Humfrey Wanley onwards. The most recent edition and discussion are in Willoughby and Ramsay, *Secular Cathedrals*, SC19.

107. T.A.M. Bishop, *English Caroline Minuscule* (Oxford, 1971), no. 9; Bishop, 'Notes on Cambridge Manuscripts, Part IV: MSS Connected with St Augustine's Canterbury', *Transactions of the Cambridge Bibliographical Society* 2 (1954–58), pp. 323–36. For Leofric as the builder of the library, see P.W. Conner, *Anglo-Saxon Exeter: A Tenth-Century Cultural History* (Woodbridge, 1993), pp. 1–20; R. Gameson, 'The Origin of the Exeter Book of Old English Poetry', *Anglo-Saxon England* 25 (1996), pp. 135–85; J. Hill, 'Leofric of Exeter and the Practical Politics of Book Collecting', in S. Kelly and J.J. Thompson (eds), *Imagining the Book* (Turnhout, 2005), pp. 77–98; and E.M. Treharne, 'Producing a Library in Late Anglo-Saxon England: Exeter, 1050–1072', *Review of English Studies*, NS, 54 (2003), pp. 155–72.

108. The principal discussion of Leofric's scribes remains that by Elaine M. Drage, 'Bishop Leofric and the Exeter Cathedral Chapter, 1050–1072: A Reassessment of the Manuscript Evidence', D.Phil. thesis (University of Oxford, 1978).

109. R. Gameson, 'Manuscrits normands à Exeter aux XIe au XIIe siècles', in *Manuscrits et enluminures dans le monde normand (Xe–XVe siècles)*, ed. M. Dosdat and P. Bouet (Caen, 1999), pp. 107–27, and M. Gullick, 'Manuscrits et copistes normands en Angleterre (XIe–XIIe siècles)', in the same volume, pp. 85–95; also C.F.R. de Hamel, *Meetings with Remarkable Manuscripts* (London, 2016), pp. 232–79.

110. See above, n. 67.

111. Most recently, Samu Niskanen, 'William of Malmesbury as Librarian: The Evidence of his Autographs', in Rodney M. Thomson, Emily Dolmans and Emily A. Winkler (eds), *Discovering William of Malmesbury* (Woodbridge, 2017), pp. 117–27.

112. On Cistercian manuscript decoration, see A. Lawrence, 'English Cistercian Manuscripts of the Twelfth Century', in C. Norton and D. Park (eds), *Cistercian Art and Architecture in the British Isles* (Cambridge, 1986), pp. 284–98; and Lawrence, 'Cistercian Decoration: Twelfth-Century Legislation on Illumination and Its Interpretation in England', *Reading Medieval Studies* 21 (1995), pp. 31–52. On Ralph of Coggeshall, see James Willoughby, 'A Templar Chronicle of the Third Crusade: Origin and Transmission', *Medium Ævum* 81 (2012), pp. 126–34, and 'The Chronicle of Ralph of Coggeshall: Publication and Censorship in Angevin England', in *The Art of Publication from the Ninth to the Sixteenth Centuries*, ed. Samu Niskanen with

the assistance of Valentina Rovere (Turnhout, forthcoming); on Cistercian writers in general, see David N. Bell, *An Index of Cistercian Authors and Works in Medieval Library Catalogues in Great Britain* (Kalamazoo MI, 1994).

113. As was argued in the last chapter of Robert Easting and Richard Sharpe, *Peter of Cornwall's Book of Revelations* (Toronto and Oxford, 2013).

114. Reginald of Durham, *Vita S. Godrici*, ed. J. Stevenson, *Libellus de vita et miraculis S. Godrici, heremitae de Finchale*, Surtees Society, 20 (1847); see further M. Coombe, 'Reginald of Durham's Latin Life of St. Godric of Finchale: A Study', D.Phil. thesis (University of Oxford, 2011); and *Reginald of Durham's Life of St Godric: An Old French Version*, ed. M. Coombe, T. Hunt and A. Mouron, Anglo-Norman Text Society, Occasional Publications, 9 (Oxford, 2019).

115. History of the Abbey of Evesham, III.1, §149; *Thomas of Marlborough, History of the Abbey of Evesham*, ed. Jane E. Sayers and Leslie Watkiss (Oxford, 2003), p. 152. Graham Pollard cites the instance of Michael of Ludgate Hill in London, known *c.*1223 as one *qui vendit libros* and twenty years later as a *venditor librorum* ('The Company of Stationers Before 1557', *The Library*, 4th series, 18 (1937–8), pp. 1–38, at p. 5).

116. Graham Pollard, 'William de Brailles', *Bodleian Library Record* 5 (1956), pp. 202–9; and Claire Donovan, *The de Brailes Hours: Shaping the Book of Hours in Thirteenth-Century Oxford* (London, 1991), with a very long list of examples, surely not all de Brailes, but generally contributing to the idea of a centre; also M.A. Michael, 'Urban Production of Manuscript Books and the Role of the University Towns', in *Cambridge History of the Book in Britain*, vol. 2, ed. Morgan and Thomson, pp. 168–94, at p. 175.

117. Parkes, 'Provision of Books', pp. 462–70.

118. Robert Grosseteste had served as *lector* in theology at the Oxford Franciscan *studium* between 1231 and 1235. The best discussion remains R.W. Hunt, 'The Library of Robert Grosseteste', in D.A. Callus (ed.), *Robert Grosseteste, Scholar and Bishop* (Oxford, 1955), pp. 121–45. On the library of the Grey Friars, see now Ralph Hanna, 'Lost Libraries: The Case of the Oxford Franciscans, *c.*1330–40', *Journal of the Early Book Society* 24 (2021), pp. 36–60.

119. See James P. Carley, 'The Dispersal of the Monastic Libraries and the Salvaging of the Spoils', in *Cambridge History of Libraries in Britain and Ireland*, vol. 1, ed. Leedham-Green and Webber, pp. 265–91, at p. 268.

120. It is also the case that the Oxford friars seem to have made gifts of some of their manuscripts in the fifteenth century. Thomas Gascoigne, that prolific reader and annotator of Oxford books, had some in his possession; see N.R. Ker, 'Oxford College Libraries before 1500', in J. Ijsewijn and J. Paquet (eds), *The Universities in the Late Middle Ages* (Louvain, 1978), pp. 293–311; repr. in Ker, *Books, Collectors and Libraries*, pp. 301–20, at p. 315; and Ball, *Thomas*

Gascoigne, Libraries, and Scholarship. See also, on William Woodford's fourteenth-century defence of the closed library, Richard H. and Mary A. Rouse, 'The Franciscans and Books: Lollard Accusations and the Franciscan Response', in Anne Hudson and Michael Wilks (eds), *From Ockham to Wyclif*, Studies in Church History, Subsidia, 5 (Oxford, 1987), pp. 369–84.

121. Richard Sharpe, 'Monastic Reading at Thorney Abbey (1323–1347)', *Traditio* 60 (2005), pp. 243–78.
122. Ibid.
123. See above, p. 65.
124. Barker-Benfield, *St Augustine's*, pp. 1841–4, discusses his collection and considers a range of candidates for identification with this monk.
125. Noted and set in context by Richard Sharpe, 'Peoples and Languages in Eleventh- and Twelfth-Century Britain and Ireland: Reading the Charter Evidence', in Dauvit Broun (ed.), *The Reality behind Charter Diplomatic in Anglo-Norman Britain* (Glasgow, 2011), pp. 1–119, at p. 65n.
126. The subject is still entwined with the foundational work of J.W. Clark, *The Care of Books* (Cambridge, 1901); also B.H. Streeter, *The Chained Library* (London, 1931). For a concise statement, see R. Gameson, 'The Medieval Library (to *c.*1450)', in *Cambridge History of Libraries in Britain and Ireland*, vol. 1, ed. Leedham-Green and Webber, pp. 13–50, at pp. 35–8. The best preserved medieval lectern desks in England are the three at Lincoln Cathedral, double-sided with generous reading slopes with an iron rod running above the ridge for the attachment of the chains. Each lectern had a pair of benches attached, one on either side. For a fuller description, see Willoughby and Ramsay, *Secular Cathedrals*. The chained library at Hereford, the most famous surviving example, dates from the seventeenth century; see F.C. Morgan, *Hereford Cathedral Library (Including the Chained Library): Its History and Contents* (Hereford, 1952; rev. edn 1973); J. Williams, 'The Library', in G.E. Aylmer and J. Tiller (eds), *Hereford Cathedral: A History* (London, 2000), pp. 511–35.
127. See Barker-Benfield, *St Augustine's*, pp. 3–7.
128. See R.W. Southern, 'From Schools to University', in *The History of the University of Oxford*, Volume 1: *The Early Oxford Schools*, ed. J.I. Catto (Oxford, 1984), pp. 1–36, at pp. 5–7, 13–14.
129. See further Willoughby, 'The *Secundo Folio* and its Uses'.
130. Statute 1 Edward VI c. 14, 'An Acte wherby certaine Chauntries Colleges Free Chapelles and the Possessions of the same be given to the Kinges Maieste'; *Statutes of the Realm*, 4 (London, 1819), pp. 24–33. The university colleges were exempted from the terms of the second Chantries Act of 1547, in an eleventh-hour amendment organized by Archbishop Thomas Cranmer. Eton and Winchester, as sister foundations to university colleges,

were included in the exemption, as was the royal foundation of St George's Chapel. All other collegiate churches fell legally forfeit to the Crown at Easter 1548; see further Willoughby, *Collegiate Churches*, pp. lxxx–lxxxi. For general discussion, see A. Kreider, *English Chantries: The Road to Dissolution* (Cambridge MA, 1979).

131. Gillespie, *Syon Abbey*, pp. 679–95.
132. A perception horizon has been fixed for the London trade by the lateness of the evidence; Paul Christianson, *Directory of London Stationers and Book Artisans, 1300–1500*, did not judge it worthwhile to look further back than 1300 for the sparse early evidence, for which see the summary by Michael, 'Urban Production of Manuscript Books', pp. 184–5.
133. Lapidge, 'Surviving Book-Lists', pp. 50–52.
134. *Rolls of the Justices in Eyre for Lincolnshire and Worcestershire*, ed. D.M. Stenton, Selden Society, 53 (1934), p. 574, no. 1167.
135. Another example might be added from the same period, *c.*1240, when Robert Grosseteste arranged for books to be purchased for his cathedral library at Lincoln from an obscure rector, John de Foxton; the bishop wrote to John offering to buy the books whatever their price. Thirty-three books duly arrived at the cathedral, where record was made of their titles in one of their number, a glossed psalter which is still in the library, MS. 139. See further Willoughby and Ramsay, *Secular Cathedrals*, SC64.
136. For orientation, see Carley, 'Dispersal of the Monastic Libraries', pp. 265–91; and Sharpe, 'Dissolution and Dispersal in Sixteenth-Century England'.
137. N.L. Ramsay, '"The Manuscripts flew about like Butterflies": The Break-up of English Libraries in the Sixteenth Century', in James Raven (ed.), *Lost Libraries: The Destruction of Great Book Collections since Antiquity* (Basingstoke, 2004), pp. 125–44.
138. See further W.A. Pantin, *Canterbury College, Oxford*, 4 vols, Oxford Historical Society, NS, 6–8, 30 (Oxford, 1947–85).
139. N.R. Ker, *Fragments of Medieval Manuscripts used as Pastedowns in Oxford Bindings. With a Survey of Oxford Binding c.1515–1620*, Oxford Bibliographical Society, NS, 5 (Oxford, 1954); repr. with additions and corrections by D. Rundle and S. Mandelbrote, Oxford Bibliographical Society, 3rd series, 4 (Oxford, 2004 for 2000). Dr Rundle has an online edition in hand.
140. J.C.T. Oates, *Cambridge University Library, A History: From the Beginnings to the Copyright Act of Queen Anne* (Cambridge, 1986), pp. 73, 87; Roger Lovatt's Introduction to P.D. Clarke, *The University and College Libraries of Cambridge*, CBMLC, 10 (London, 2002), p. lxxxviii.
141. Ralph Hanna and David Rundle, *A Descriptive Catalogue of the Western Manuscripts, to c.1600, in Christ Church, Oxford*, Oxford Bibliographical

Society Publications, Special Series, Manuscript Catalogues, 2 (Oxford, 2017), pp. 30, 39. On the crisis for libraries in the early sixteenth century, see further N.R. Ker, 'Oxford College Libraries in the Sixteenth Century', *Bodleian Library Record* 6 (1957–61), pp. 459–515; repr. in Ker, *Books, Collectors and Libraries*, pp. 379–436.

142. G. Powitz, '*Libri inutiles* in mittelalterlichen Bibliotheken. Bemerkungen über Alienatio, Palimpsestierung und Makulierung', *Scriptorium* 50 (1996), pp. 288–304.

143. The library which Cardinal Wolsey intended for his Oxford foundation of Cardinal College requires mention at this point: he made a large request among his friends in the papal curia for Greek exemplars and scribes to copy them. Catalogues were drawn up for him of suitable books in the Vatican Library and the Marciana in Venice. He was envisaging in the later 1520s a college library on a different scale and with a new temper than those Professor Sharpe is discussing here. See James Willoughby, 'Thomas Wolsey and the Books of Cardinal College, Oxford', *Bodleian Library Record* 28 (2015), pp. 114–34. Another way in which Wolsey stands as an exception is in his preference for manuscript over print for de luxe books, as represented by his surviving twin lectionaries; see David Rundle, *The Renaissance Reform of the Book and Britain: The English Quattrocento* (Cambridge, 2019), pp. 143, 146.

144. David McKitterick, *Print, Manuscript, and the Search for Order, 1450–1830* (Cambridge, 2003), pp. 12–13, giving the examples of the Bodleian Library and Leiden University.

145. William Farrer, *The Chartulary of Cockersand Abbey of the Premonstratensian Order*, 3 vols in 7, Chetham Society, NS, pp. 38–40, 43, 56–7, 64 (Manchester, 1898–1909), vol. 3, p. 1171. The document is The National Archives, PRO, Duchy of Lancaster: Rentals and Surveys, DL 43/5/5.

146. Further discussion in Claire Cross, 'Monastic Learning and Libraries in Sixteenth-Century Yorkshire', in J. Kirk (ed.), *Humanism and Reform: The Church in Europe, England, and Scotland, 1400–1643. Essays in Honour of James K. Cameron*, Studies in Church History, Subsidia, 8 (Oxford, 1991), pp. 255–69; and Carley, 'Dispersal of the Monastic Libraries', pp. 284–5. Cross, 'A Medieval Yorkshire Library', *Northern History* 25 (1989), pp. 281–90, makes a case for a similar evacuation of library books from the Yorkshire abbey of Byland.

147. Liddell, '"Leland"'s List of Manuscripts in Lincolnshire Monasteries', pp. 88–95. The inverted commas around Leland's name show that Liddell already questioned what had been an assumption made by those who had cited this collection of lists, namely that they resulted from John Leland's researches on behalf of King Henry VIII before 1536.

148. Carley, *Henry VIII*, pp. xxxiii–xxxv, lxii n. 198.
149. The library room at the cathedral was built on the first floor of the cloister, with a row of two-light windows on the east and west walls, one window to each bay and larger, five-light windows at each end. The room's five-bay structure would have allowed for eight lecterns running out from the walls between the lights, four on each side of the room. Exceptionally, three of these lecterns are still on the spot: see above, n. 126.
150. Bateson, *Catalogue of Syon*, p. xx: 'I began to copy the manuscript out of mere curiosity, with scarcely a suspicion of the countless bibliographical pitfalls into which I was walking, for the whole of the land was to me undiscovered country.'
151. V.A. Gillespie, *Syon Abbey*, CBMLC, 9 (London, 2001).
152. Injunctions issued by Edward VI in 1547 required every cathedral to have a library of patristic theology, with the works of Saints Augustine, Basil, Gregory Nazianzen, Jerome, Ambrose, John Chrysostom, Cyprian and Theophylact, as well as of Erasmus; see W.H. Frere and W.M. Kennedy, *Visitation Articles and Injunctions of the Period of the Reformation*, 3 vols, Alcuin Club Collections 14–16 (London, 1910), vol. 1, p. 135, vol. 2, p. 136. The exiguous evidence for chapter libraries at the cathedrals of New Foundation are set out in Willoughby and Ramsay, *Secular Cathedrals*. A visitation of Gloucester cathedral in 1548 included a question as to whether the king's statutes and injunctions had been observed. The subdean admitted in reply that 'librarium et libros in eodem contentos hucusque plenarie non acquisivimus, adhibita tamen diligentia qua nonnullos obtinuimus'; W.D. Macray, 'Manuscripts of the Diocese of Gloucester', *HMC 8th Report* (1911), p. 49.
153. See Tuomas Heikkilä, 'The Fate of the Medieval Libraries in the Swedish Realm during the Reformation', in *How the Secularization of Religious Houses Transformed the Libraries of Europe* (forthcoming). Those Swedish binding leaves may now be analysed as manuscripts, and are found to offer a better testimony to ordinary English twelfth-century liturgical books than have survived anywhere in England. See Kerstin Abukhanfusa, *Mutilated Books: Wondrous Leaves from Swedish Bibliographical History* (Stockholm, 2004); and Michael Gullick, 'Preliminary Observations on Romanesque Manuscript Fragments of English, Norman and Swedish Origin in the Riksarkivet (Stockholm)', in Jan Brunius (ed.), *Medieval Book Fragments in Sweden: An International Seminar in Stockholm, 13–16 November 2003* (Stockholm, 2005), pp. 31–82.
154. See above, pp. 121–2.
155. De Hamel, 'Dispersal of the Library of Christ Church, Canterbury'.
156. Ker, 'Migration of Manuscripts'.

157. The suggestion, suitably hedged around here, that nunneries might have played a larger role in helping to preserve vernacular literature does not really hold with the evidence from *MLGB*, in which 32 of 214 books containing works in English and 9 out of 78 French books are provenanced to female houses. That suggests a higher per capita rate of vernacular reading in female institutions than in male, but it still represents a minority culture.

158. I have been unable to fasten a reference to Professor Sharpe's mention of Bradshaw's paradox, although the significance of it is plain enough. David McKitterick has pointed out to us Bradshaw's presidential address to the Library Association in 1882, which bears repeating in this context. There, Bradshaw spoke of different kinds of libraries, hierarchically arranged with research libraries at the top. 'When the antiquarian element becomes developed in the library, a higher stage still is reached. By this I mean, what I must be allowed to consider a higher stage in the character and usefulness of a library. To any one engaged in historical research upon any subject it soon becomes manifest that this destruction of obsolete books which our forefathers encouraged, led to the result, which we their successors now find so inconvenient, that any books which alone contain certain pieces of much desired information, have come down to us in single copies, or at best in copies preserved in some half-dozen widely scattered libraries.... Hence arises a new demand. The library which in the lower stages which I have noticed already, contained nothing but common books to serve the purpose of its habitual frequenters, becomes more and more, as its contents are better known, an object of pilgrimage to students living at a distance.... Thus it is that by the existence of this antiquarian element in its composition, whether of old printed books or manuscripts, the library acquires prestige which in its earlier stages it could never have possessed.' ('The President's Address to the Opening of the Fifth Annual Meeting of the Library Association of the United Kingdom, Cambridge, SE pt. 5, 1882', in *Collected Papers of Henry Bradshaw*, ed. F. Jenkinson (Cambridge, 1889), pp. 371–4, at pp. 375–6.)

Select Bibliography

Abukhanfusa, K., *Mutilated Books: Wondrous Leaves from Swedish Bibliographical History* (Stockholm, 2004).

Adams, J., 'Thomas Hunt's Monograms', *The Library*, 7th series, 22 (2021), pp. 376–82.

Álvarez López, F.L., and J.C. Crick, 'Decision-Making and Work Flow in the Making of Exon Domesday', in B.A. Shailor and C. Dutschke (eds), *Scribes and the Presentation of Texts (from Antiquity to c. 1550): Proceedings of the 20th Colloquium of the Comité international de paléographie latine* (Turnhout, 2021), pp. 155–75.

Bainbridge, V.R., 'Syon Abbey: Women and Learning *c.* 1415–1600', in E.A. Jones and A. Walsham (eds), *Syon Abbey and its Books: Reading, Writing and Religion, c. 1400–1700* (Woodbridge, 2010), pp. 82–103.

Bale, J., *Scriptorum illustrium Maioris Brytanniae catalogus*, 2nd edn, 2 pts (Apud Ioannem Oporinum, Basel, 1557–59).

Ball, R.M., *Thomas Gascoigne, Libraries and Scholarship*, Cambridge Bibliographical Society Monographs 14 (Cambridge, 2006).

Barker-Benfield, B.C., *St Augustine's Abbey, Canterbury*, CBMLC, 13, 3 vols (London, 2008).

Bartlett, R. (ed.), *Life and Miracles of St Modwenna* (Oxford, 2002).

Bateson, M., *Catalogue of the Library of Syon Monastery Isleworth* (Cambridge, 1898).

Bell, D.N., *An Index of Cistercian Authors and Works in Medieval Library Catalogues in Great Britain* (Kalamazoo MI, 1994).

Binski, P., and S. Panayotova (eds), *The Cambridge Illuminations: Ten Centuries of Book Production in the Medieval West* (London, 2005).

Bishop, T.A.M., 'Notes on Cambridge Manuscripts, Part IV: MSS Connected with St Augustine's Canterbury', *Transactions of the Cambridge Bibliographical Society* 2 (1954–58), pp. 323–36.

———, *English Caroline Minuscule* (Oxford, 1971).

[Botfield, B.], *Catalogi veteres ecclesiae cathedralis Dunelmensis*, Surtees Society 1 (1838).

Bradshaw, H., *Collected Papers of Henry Bradshaw*, ed. F. Jenkinson (Cambridge, 1889).

Buringh, E., 'The Role of Medieval Cities in Book Production: Quantitative Analyses', in *Uses of the Written Word in Medieval Towns: Medieval Urban Literacy II*, ed. M. Mostert and A. Adamska (Turnhout, 2014), pp. 119–77.

———, 'Loss Rates of Medieval English and Scottish Books', forthcoming.

Burtt, J., 'Notes Upon Ancient Libraries', *Notes & Queries* 1 (1849), pp. 21–3.

Carley, J.P., and C.G.C. Tite (eds), *Books and Collectors 1200–1700: Essays presented to Andrew Watson* (London, 1997), pp. 263–79.

———, *The Libraries of King Henry VIII*, CBMLC, 7 (London, 2000).

———, 'The Dispersal of the Monastic Libraries and the Salvaging of the Spoils', in *A History of Libraries in Britain and Ireland*, Volume 1: *From the Beginnings to 1640*, ed. E.S. Leedham-Green and M.T.J. Webber (Cambridge, 2006), pp. 265–91.

———, *John Leland, De viris illustribus. On Famous Men* (Toronto and Oxford, 2010).

Christianson, C.P., *A Directory of London Stationers and Book Artisans, 1300–1500* (New York, 1990).

Clark, J.W., *The Observances in Use at the Augustinian Priory of S. Giles and S. Andrew at Barnwell, Cambridgeshire* (Cambridge, 1897).

———, *The Care of Books* (Cambridge, 1901).

Clarke, P.D., *The University and College Libraries of Cambridge*, CBMLC, 10 (London, 2002).

Coates, A., *English Medieval Books: The Reading Abbey Collections from Foundation to Dispersal* (Oxford, 1999).

———, and K. Jensen, C. Dondi and others, *A Catalogue of Books Printed in the Fifteenth Century now in the Bodleian Library*, 6 vols (Oxford, 2005).

Conner, P.W., *Anglo-Saxon Exeter: A Tenth-Century Cultural History* (Woodbridge, 1993).

Coombe, M., 'Reginald of Durham's Latin Life of St. Godric of Finchale: A Study', D.Phil. thesis (University of Oxford, 2011).

———, and T. Hunt and A. Mouron (eds), *Reginald of Durham's Life of St Godric: An Old French Version*, Anglo-Norman Text Society, Occasional Publications 9 (2019).

Cross, C., 'A Medieval Yorkshire Library', *Northern History* 25 (1989), pp. 281–90.

———, 'Monastic Learning and Libraries in Sixteenth-Century Yorkshire', in J. Kirk (ed.), *Humanism and Reform: The Church in Europe, England, and Scotland, 1400–1643. Essays in Honour of James K. Cameron*, Studies in Church History, Subsidia 8 (Oxford, 1991), pp. 255–69.

Dondi, C., D. Raines and R. Sharpe (eds), *How the Secularization of Religious Houses Transformed the Libraries of Europe, 16th–19th Centuries* (Turnhout, forthcoming).

Donovan, C., *The de Brailes Hours: Shaping the Book of Hours in Thirteenth-Century Oxford* (London, 1991).

Doyle, A.I., 'The Printed Books of the Last Monks of Durham', *The Library*, 7th series, 10 (1988), pp. 203–19.

———, *The Libraries of the Carthusians*, CBMLC, 9 (London, 2001).

Drage, E.M., 'Bishop Leofric and the Exeter Cathedral Chapter, 1050–1072: A Reassessment of the Manuscript Evidence', D.Phil. thesis (University of Oxford, 1978).

Easting, R., and R. Sharpe, *Peter of Cornwall's Book of Revelations* (Toronto and Oxford, 2013).

Edwards, A.S.G., and S. Horobin, 'Further Books Annotated by Stephen Batman', *The Library*, 7th series, 11 (2010), pp. 227–31.

Emden, A.B., *A Biographical Register of the University of Oxford to A.D. 1500*, 3 vols (Oxford, 1957–59).

Farrer, W., *The Chartulary of Cockersand Abbey of the Premonstratensian Order*, 3 vols in 7, Chetham Society, NS, 38–40, 43, 56–7, 64 (Manchester, 1898–1909).

Frere, W.H., and W.M. Kennedy, *Visitation Articles and Injunctions of the Period of the Reformation*, 3 vols, Alcuin Club Collections 14–16 (London, 1910).

Friis-Jensen, K., and J.M.W. Willoughby, *Peterborough Abbey*, CBMLC, 8 (London, 2001).

Gameson, R., 'The Origin of the Exeter Book of Old English Poetry', *Anglo-Saxon England* 25 (1996), pp. 135–85.

———, 'Manuscrits normands à Exeter aux XIe au XIIe siècles', in *Manuscrits et enluminures dans le monde normand (X^e–XVe siècles)*, ed. M. Dosdat and P. Bouet (Caen, 1999), pp. 107–27.

———, 'The Medieval Library (to *c.* 1450)', in *A History of Libraries in Britain and Ireland*, Volume 1: *From the Beginnings to 1640*, ed. E.S. Leedham-Green and M.T.J. Webber (Cambridge, 2006), pp. 13–50.

———, 'The Circulation of Books Between England and the Continent, *c.* 871–*c.* 1100', in *The Cambridge History of the Book in Britain*, Volume 1: *c. 400–1100*, ed. R. Gameson (Cambridge, 2011), pp. 344–72.

———, *The Medieval Manuscripts of Trinity College, Oxford: A Descriptive Catalogue*, Oxford Bibliographical Society Publications, Special Series, Manuscript Catalogues 3 (Oxford, 2018).

Gesta abbatum monasterii Sancti Albani, ed. H.T. Riley, Rolls Series 28, 3 vols (London, 1867–69).

Gillespie, V.A., *Syon Abbey*, CBMLC, 9 (London, 2001).

Gneuss, H., and M. Lapidge, *Anglo-Saxon Manuscripts: A Bibliographical Handlist of Manuscripts and Manuscript Fragments Written or Owned in England up to 1100* (Toronto, 2014).

Greatrex, J., *The English Benedictine Cathedral Priories: Rule and Practice* (Oxford, 2011).

Gullick, M., 'The Scribe of the Carilef Bible: A New Look at Some Late-Eleventh-Century Durham Cathedral Manuscripts', in Linda L. Brownrigg (ed.), *Medieval Book Production: Assessing the Evidence. Proceedings of the Second Conference of the Seminar in the History of the Book to 1500, Oxford, July 1988* (Los Altos Hills CA, 1990), pp. 61–83.

———, 'The Scribal Work of Eadmer of Canterbury to 1109', *Archaeologia Cantiana* 118 (1998), pp. 173–89.

———, 'Manuscrits et copistes normands en Angleterre (XIe–XIIe siècles)', in *Manuscrits et enluminures dans le monde normand (X^e–XVe siècles)*, ed. M. Dosdat and P. Bouet (Caen, 1999), pp. 85–95.

———, 'Preliminary Observations on Romanesque Manuscript Fragments of English, Norman and Swedish Origin in the Riksarkivet (Stockholm)', in J. Brunius (ed.), *Medieval Book Fragments in Sweden: An International Seminar in Stockholm, 13–16 November 2003* (Stockholm, 2005), pp. 31–82.

Hamel, C.F.R. de, *Syon Abbey: The Library of the Bridgettine Nuns and Their Peregrinations after the Reformation*, Roxburghe Club (Cambridge, 1991).

———, 'The Dispersal of the Library of Christ Church, Canterbury, from the Fourteenth to the Sixteenth Century', in J.P. Carley and C.G.C. Tite (eds), *Books and Collectors 1200–1700: Essays Presented to Andrew Watson* (London, 1997), pp. 263–79.

———, *Meetings with Remarkable Manuscripts* (London, 2016).

Hanna, R., 'Lost Libraries: The Case of the Oxford Franciscans, *c.* 1330–40', *Journal of the Early Book Society* 24 (2021), pp. 36–60.

———, and D.G. Rundle, *A Descriptive Catalogue of the Western Manuscripts, to c. 1600, in Christ Church, Oxford*, Oxford Bibliographical Society Publications, Special Series, Manuscript Catalogues 2 (Oxford, 2017).

Hardy, T.D., *Descriptive Catalogue of Materials Relating to the History of Great Britain and Ireland to the End of the Reign of Henry VII*, Rolls Series 26, 4 pts in 3 vols (London, 1862–71).

Heikkilä, T., 'The Fate of the Medieval Libraries in the Swedish Realm during the Reformation', in C. Dondi, D. Raines and R. Sharpe (eds), *How the Secularization of Religious Houses Transformed the Libraries of Europe, 16th–19th Centuries* (Turnhout, forthcoming).

Hickes, G., and H. Wanley, *Antiquae literaturae septentrionalis libri duo*, 2 vols (E Theatro Sheldoniano, Oxford, 1705).

Higgitt, J., with an introduction by J. Durkan, *Scottish Libraries*, CBMLC, 12 (London, 2006).

Hill, J., 'Leofric of Exeter and the Practical Politics of Book Collecting', in S. Kelly and J.J. Thompson (eds), *Imagining the Book* (Turnhout, 2005), pp. 77–98.

Horobin, S., and A. Nafde, 'Stephan Batman and the Making of the Parker Library', *Transactions of the Cambridge Bibliographical Society* 15 (2015), pp. 561–81.

Hunt, R.W., 'The Library of Robert Grosseteste', in D.A. Callus (ed.), *Robert Grosseteste, Scholar and Bishop* (Oxford, 1955), pp. 121–45.

Hunter, J., *South Yorkshire* (London, 1828–31; repr. Wakefield, 1974).

———, *English Monastic Libraries* (London, 1831).

Hutchison, A.M., '"To yowr gostly comforte and proffite": Devotional Reading for the Nuns of Syon Abbey', in V. Blanton, V. O'Mara and P. Stoop (eds), *Nuns' Literacies in Medieval Europe: The Antwerp Dialogue* (Turnhout, 2017), pp. 61–82.

James, M.R., *The Ancient Libraries of Canterbury and Dover: The Catalogues of the Libraries of Christ Church Priory and St Augustine's Abbey at Canterbury, and of St Martin's Priory at Dover* (Cambridge, 1903).

———, 'The Catalogue of the Library of the Augustinian Friars at York', in *Fasciculus Joanni Willis Clark dicatus* (Cambridge, 1909), pp. 2–96.

———, 'Lists of Manuscripts Formerly in Peterborough Abbey Library', *Transactions of the Bibliographical Society*, Supplement 5 (Oxford, 1926).

———, 'Catalogue of the Library of Leicester Abbey', *Transactions of the Leicestershire Archaeological Society* 19 (1936–7), pp. 118–61, 378–440; 21 (1939–41), pp. 1–88.

Ker, N.R., *Medieval Libraries of Great Britain*, 1st edn (London, 1941); 2nd edn (London, 1964); Supplement, ed. A.G. Watson (London, 1987); digital 3rd edn (2015), *MLGB3*, available online from the Bodleian Library, Oxford, at http://mlgb3.bodleian.ox.ac.uk.

———, 'The Migration of Manuscripts from the English Medieval Libraries', *The Library*, 4th series, 23 (1942), pp. 1–11; repr. in Ker, *Books, Collectors and Libraries: Studies in the Medieval Heritage*, ed. A.G. Watson (London, [1985]), pp. 459–70.

———, and I. Atkins (eds), *Catalogus librorum manuscriptorum bibliothecae Wigorniensis: Made in 1622–1623* (Cambridge, 1944).

———, *Catalogue of Manuscripts Containing Anglo-Saxon* (Oxford, 1957).

———, 'Medieval Manuscripts from Norwich Cathedral Priory', *Transactions of the Cambridge Bibliographical Society* 1 (1949–53), pp. 1–28; repr. in Ker, *Books, Collectors and Libraries: Studies in the Medieval Heritage*, ed. A.G. Watson (London, [1985]), pp. 243–72.

———, *Fragments of Medieval Manuscripts Used as Pastedowns in Oxford Bindings. With a Survey of Oxford Binding c. 1515–1620*, Oxford Bibliographical Society, NS,

5 (Oxford, 1954); repr. with additions and corrections by D. Rundle and S. Mandelbrote, Oxford Bibliographical Society, 3rd series, 4 (Oxford, 2004).

———, 'Oxford College Libraries in the Sixteenth Century', *Bodleian Library Record* 6 (1957–61), pp. 459–515; repr. in Ker, *Books, Collectors and Libraries: Studies in the Medieval Heritage*, ed. A.G. Watson (London, [1985]), pp. 379–436.

———, *English Manuscripts in the Century After the Norman Conquest: The Lyell Lectures 1952–3* (Oxford, 1960).

———, 'Oxford College Libraries before 1500', in J. Ijsewijn and J. Paquet (eds), *The Universities in the Late Middle Ages* (Louvain, 1978), pp. 293–311; repr. in Ker, *Books, Collectors and Libraries: Studies in the Medieval Heritage*, ed. A.G. Watson (London, [1985]), pp. 301–20.

———, *Books, Collectors and Libraries: Studies in the Medieval Heritage*, ed. A.G. Watson (London, [1985])

Keynes, S., 'King Athelstan's Books', in M. Lapidge and H. Gneuss (eds), *Learning and Literature in Anglo-Saxon England: Studies Presented to Peter Clemoes on the Occasion of his Sixty-Fifth Birthday* (Cambridge, 1985), pp. 143–201.

Knowles, D., C.N.L. Brooke and V.C.M. London, *The Heads of Religious Houses, England and Wales*, Volume 1: *940–1216* (Cambridge, 2001).

Kraebel, A.B., 'A Further Book Annotated by Stephan Batman, with New Material for His Biography', *The Library*, 7th series, 16 (2015), pp. 458–66.

Kreider, A., *English Chantries: The Road to Dissolution* (Cambridge MA, 1979).

Lapidge, M., 'Surviving Booklists from Anglo-Saxon England', in M. Lapidge and H. Gneuss (eds), *Learning and Literature in Anglo-Saxon England: Studies Presented to Peter Clemoes on the Occasion of his Sixty-Fifth Birthday* (Cambridge, 1985), pp. 33–89; rev. version in M.P. Richards (ed.), *Anglo-Saxon Manuscripts: Basic Readings* (London, 1994), pp. 87–169.

———, 'Acca of Hexham and the Origin of the *Old English Martyrology*', *Analecta Bollandiana* 123 (2005), pp. 29–78.

———, *The Anglo-Saxon Library* (Oxford, 2006).

Lawrence, A., 'English Cistercian Manuscripts of the Twelfth Century', in C. Norton and D. Park (eds), *Cistercian Art and Architecture in the British Isles* (Cambridge, 1986), pp. 284–98.

———, 'Cistercian Decoration: Twelfth-Century Legislation on Illumination and its Interpretation in England', *Reading Medieval Studies* 21 (1995), pp. 31–52.

Leland, J., *De viris illustribus*, in *John Leland, De viris illustribus. On Famous Men*, ed. J.P. Carley (Toronto and Oxford, 2010).

Liddell, J.R., '"Leland's" Lists of Manuscripts in Lincolnshire Monasteries', *English Historical Review* 54 (1939), pp. 88–95.

Macray, W.D., 'Manuscripts of the Diocese of Gloucester', Historical Manuscripts Commission, 8th *Report* (1911).

Martène, E., *De antiquis Ecclesiae ritibus libri quatuor*, 2nd edn, 3 vols (Milan, 1736–37).

McKitterick, D., *Print, Manuscript, and the Search for Order, 1450–1830* (Cambridge, 2003).

Michael, M.A., 'Urban Production of Manuscript Books and the Role of the University Towns', in *The Cambridge History of the Book in Britain*, Volume 2: *1100–1400*, ed. N.J. Morgan and R.M. Thomson (Cambridge, 2008), pp. 168–94.

Morgan, F.C., *Hereford Cathedral Library (Including the Chained Library): Its History and Contents* (Hereford, 1952; rev. edn, 1973)

Munby, A.N.L., 'Notes on King's College Library in the Fifteenth Century', *Transactions of the Cambridge Bibliographical Society*, vol. 1 (1949–53), pp. 280–86; repr. in Munby, *Essays and Papers* (London, 1977), pp. 27–36.

Mynors, R.A.B., *Durham Cathedral Manuscripts to the End of the Twelfth Century* (Oxford, 1939).

———, *Catalogue of the Manuscripts of Balliol College, Oxford* (Oxford, 1963).

Nichols, J., *The History and Antiquities of the County of Leicester*, 8 pts in 4 vols (London, for the author, 1795–1815).

Niskanen, S., 'William of Malmesbury as Librarian: The Evidence of His Autographs', in R.M. Thomson, E. Dolmans and E.A. Winkler (eds), *Discovering William of Malmesbury* (Woodbridge, 2017), pp. 117–27.

——— (ed.), *Epistolae Anselmi Cantuariensis Archiepiscopi: Letters of Anselm, Archbishop of Canterbury*, Volume 1: *The Bec Letters* (Oxford, 2019).

Oates, J.C.T., *Cambridge University Library, A History: From the Beginnings to the Copyright Act of Queen Anne* (Cambridge, 1986).

Omont, H., 'Anciens catalogues de bibliothèques anglaises', *Centralblatt für Bibliothekswesen* 9 (1892), pp. 201–22.

Pantin, W.A., *Documents Illustrating the Activities of the General and Provincial Chapters of the English Black Monks, 1215–1540*, Camden Society, 3rd series, 45, 47, 54 (1931–37).

———, *Canterbury College, Oxford*, 4 vols, Oxford Historical Society, NS, 6–8, 30 (Oxford, 1947–85).

Parkes, M.B., 'The Provision of Books', in *The History of the University of Oxford*, Volume 2: *Late Medieval Oxford*, ed. J.I. Catto and T.A.R. Evans (Oxford, 1992), pp. 407–83; repr. in Parkes, *Pages From the Past: Medieval Writing Skills and Medieval Books* (Farnham, 2012).

———, 'Stephan Batman's Manuscripts', in M. Kanno and others (eds), *Medieval Heritage: Essays in Honour of Tadahiro Ikegami* (Tokyo, 1997), pp. 125–56; repr. with addenda in P.R. Robinson and R. Zim (eds), *Pages from the Past: Medieval Writing Skills and Manuscript Books* (Farnham, 2012).

———, 'Thomas Hunt and the Oxford Book-Business in the Late Fifteenth Century', *The Library*, 7th series, 17 (2016), pp. 28–39.
Piper, A., 'The Libraries of the Monks of Durham', in M.B. Parkes and A.G. Watson (eds), *Medieval Scribes, Manuscripts and Libraries: Essays Presented to N.R. Ker* (London, 1978), pp. 213–49.
———, *The Libraries of Durham Cathedral Priory*, CBMLC, forthcoming.
Pollard, G., The Company of Stationers Before 1557', *The Library*, 4th series, 18 (1937–8), pp. 1–38.
———, 'William de Brailles', *Bodleian Library Record* 5 (1956), pp. 202–9.
Powitz, G., '*Libri inutiles* in mittelalterlichen Bibliotheken. Bemerkungen über Alienatio, Palimpsestierung und Makulierung', *Scriptorium* 50 (1996), pp. 288–304.
Ramsay, N.L., '"The Manuscripts flew about like Butterflies": The Break-up of English Libraries in the Sixteenth Century', in J. Raven (ed.), *Lost Libraries: The Destruction of Great Book Collections Since Antiquity* (Basingstoke, 2004), pp. 125–44.
———, 'Law', in *The Cambridge History of the Book in Britain*, Volume 2: *1100–1400*, ed. N.J. Morgan and R.M. Thomson (Cambridge, 2008), pp. 250–90.
———, and J.M.W. Willoughby, *Hospitals, Towns, and the Professions*, CBMLC, 14 (London, 2009).
Reginald of Durham, *Vita S. Godrici*, in *Libellus de vita et miraculis S. Godrici, heremitae de Finchale*, ed. J. Stevenson, Surtees Society 20 (1847).
Rouse, R.H., and M.A. Rouse, 'The Franciscans and Books: Lollard Accusations and the Franciscan Response', in Anne Hudson and Michael Wilks (eds), *From Ockham to Wyclif*, Studies in Church History, Subsidia 5 (Oxford, 1987), pp. 369–84.
———, *Registrum Anglie de libris doctorum et auctorum veterum*, CBMLC, 2 (London, 1991).
———, *Henry of Kirkestede, Catalogus de libris autenticis et apocrifis*, CBMLC, 11 (London, 2004).
Rundle, D.G., *The Renaissance Reform of the Book and Britain: The English Quattrocento* (Cambridge, 2019).
SanPietro, I., 'The Making of a Christian Intellectual Tradition in Jerome's *De viris illustribus*', *Memoirs of the American Academy in Rome* 62 (2017), pp. 231–60.
Sayers, J.E., and L. Watkiss (eds), *Thomas of Marlborough: History of the Abbey of Evesham* (Oxford, 2003).
Sharpe, R., 'Accession, Classification, or Location. Pressmarks in Medieval Libraries', *Scriptorium* 50 (1996), pp. 279–87.
———, and J.P. Carley, R.M. Thomson and A.G. Watson, *English Benedictine Libraries: The Shorter Catalogues*, CBMLC, 4 (London, 1996).

———, *A Handlist of the Latin Writers of Great Britain and Ireland before 1540* (Turnhout, 1997).

———, 'Reconstructing the Medieval Library of Bury St Edmunds: The Lost Catalogue of Henry of Kirkstead', in A. Gransden (ed.), *Bury St Edmunds: Medieval Art, Architecture, Archaeology, and Economy*, British Archaeological Association, Conference Transactions 1994 ([Leeds], 1998), pp. 204–18.

———, *Titulus. Identifying Medieval Latin Texts: An Evidence-Based Approach* (Turnhout, 2003).

———, 'Monastic Reading at Thorney Abbey (1323–1347)', *Traditio* 60 (2005), pp. 243–78.

———, 'The Medieval Librarian', in *A History of Libraries in Britain and Ireland*, Volume 1: *From the Beginnings to 1640*, ed. E.S. Leedham-Green and M.T.J. Webber (Cambridge, 2006), pp. 218–41.

———, 'Library Catalogues and Indexes', in *The Cambridge History of the Book in Britain*, Volume 2: *1100–1400*, ed. N.J. Morgan and R.M. Thomson (Cambridge, 2008), pp. 197–218.

———, 'Henry Ellis, Richard Gough's Protégé', *Bodleian Library Record* 22 (2009), 191–211.

———, 'Peoples and Languages in Eleventh- and Twelfth-Century Britain and Ireland: Reading the Charter Evidence', in D. Broun (ed.), *The Reality behind Charter Diplomatic in Anglo-Norman Britain* (Glasgow, 2011), pp. 1–119.

———, 'Dissolution and Dispersal in Sixteenth-Century England: Understanding the Remains', in C. Dondi, D. Raines and R. Sharpe (eds), *How the Secularization of Religious Houses Transformed the Libraries of Europe, 16th–19th Centuries* (Turnhout, forthcoming).

Sheppard, J.B., *Literae Cantuarienses: The Letter Books of the Monastery of Christ Church, Canterbury*, Rolls Series 85 (London, 1887–89).

Sheppard, J.M., *The Buildwas Books: Book Production, Acquisition and Use at an English Cistercian Monastery, 1165–c.1400*, Oxford Bibliographical Society Publications, 3rd series, 2 (Oxford, 1997).

Smalley, B., 'A Collection of Paris Lectures of the Later Twelfth Century in the MS. Pembroke College, Cambridge 7', *Cambridge Historical Journal* 6 (1938), pp. 103–13.

Smith, D.M., and V.C.M. London, *The Heads of Religious Houses, England and Wales*, Volume 2: *1216-1377* (Cambridge, 2001).

Southern, R.W., 'From Schools to University', in *The History of the University of Oxford*, Volume 1: *The Early Oxford Schools*, ed. J.I. Catto (Oxford, 1984), pp. 1–36.

Statuta antiqua universitatis Oxoniensis, ed. Strickland Gibson (Oxford, 1931), pp. 183–7.

Steele, M.W., 'A Study of the Books Owned or Used by John Grandisson, Bishop of Exeter', D.Phil. thesis (University of Oxford, 1994).
Stokes, P.A. (ed.), *Exon: The Domesday Survey of South-West England*, Studies in Domesday, gen. ed. J.C. Crick (London, 2018).
Streeter, B.H., *The Chained Library* (London, 1931).
Thompson, E.M. (ed.), *Customary of the Benedictine Monasteries of St Augustine, Canterbury, and St Peter, Westminster*, 2 vols, Henry Bradshaw Society 23, 28 (London, 1902–4).
Thomson, R.M., *A Descriptive Catalogue of the Medieval Manuscripts in Worcester Cathedral Library* (Cambridge, 2001).
———, *Books and Learning in Twelfth-Century England: The Ending of 'alter orbis'. The Lyell Lectures 2000–2001* (Walkern, 2006).
———, *A Descriptive Catalogue of the Medieval Manuscripts of Merton College, Oxford* (Cambridge, 2009).
———, 'William Reed, Bishop of Chichester (d. 1385) – Bibliophile?', in G.H. Brown and L.E. Voigts (eds), *The Study of Medieval Manuscripts of England: Festschrift in Honor of Richard W. Pfaff* (Tempe AZ, 2010), pp. 281–93.
Tolhurst, J.B.L. (ed.), *The Ordinale and Customary of the Benedictine Nuns of Barking Abbey: (University College, Oxford, MS. 169)*, 2 vols, Henry Bradshaw Society 65–6 (London, 1927–8).
Treharne, E.M., 'Producing a Library in Late Anglo-Saxon England: Exeter, 1050–1072', *Review of English Studies*, NS, 54 (2003), pp. 155–72.
Vincent, N.C., *The Letters and Charters of Cardinal Guala Bicchieri, 1216–1218*, Canterbury & York Society 83 (1996).
Wansbrough, H., and A. Marett-Crosby (eds.), *Benedictines in Oxford* (London, 1997).
Watson, A.G., 'John Twyne of Canterbury (d. 1581) as a Collector of Medieval Manuscripts: A Preliminary Investigation', *The Library*, 6th series, 8 (1986), pp. 133–51.
Webber, T., *Scribes and Scholars at Salisbury Cathedral, c. 1075–c. 1125* (Oxford, 1992).
———, 'Script and Manuscript Production at Christ Church, Canterbury, after the Norman Conquest', in R. Eales and R. Sharpe (eds), *Canterbury and the Norman Conquest: Churches, Saints, and Scholars 1066–1109* (London, 1995), pp. 145–58.
———, and A.G. Watson, *The Libraries of the Augustinian Canons*, CBMLC, 6 (London, 1998).
———, 'Monastic and Cathedral Book Collections in the Late Eleventh and Twelfth Centuries', in *A History of Libraries in Britain and Ireland*, Volume 1: *From the Beginnings to 1640*, ed. E.S. Leedham-Green and M.T.J. Webber (Cambridge, 2006), pp. 109–25.

Williams, J., 'The Library', in G.E. Aylmer and J. Tiller (eds), *Hereford Cathedral: A History* (London, 2000), pp. 511–35.
Willoughby, J.M.W., 'The *Secundo Folio* and its Uses, Medieval and Modern', *The Library*, 7th series, 12 (2011), pp. 237–58.
———, 'Common Libraries in Fifteenth-Century England: An Episcopal Benefaction', in V.A. Gillespie and K. Ghosh (eds), *After Arundel: Religious Writing in Fifteenth-Century England* (Turnhout, 2011), pp. 209–22.
———, 'A Templar Chronicle of the Third Crusade: Origin and Transmission', *Medium Ævum* 81 (2012), pp. 126–34.
———, *The Libraries of Collegiate Churches*, CBMLC, 15 (London, 2013).
———, 'Thomas Wolsey and the Books of Cardinal College, Oxford', *Bodleian Library Record* 28 (2015), pp. 114–34.
———, 'The Transmission and Circulation of Classical Literature: Libraries and Florilegia', in *The Oxford History of Classical Reception in English Literature*, Volume 1: *800–1558*, ed. R. Copeland (Oxford, 2016), pp. 98–101.
———, 'Cardinal Marcello Cervini (1501–1555) and English Libraries', in J.M.W. Willoughby and J.I. Catto (eds), *Books and Bookmen in Early Modern Britain: Essays Presented to James P. Carley* (Toronto, 2018), pp. 119–49.
———, 'Italian Evidence for Duke Humfrey's Library before its Dispersal', *Bodleian Library Record* 31 (2018), pp. 20–30.
———, and N.L. Ramsay, *The Libraries of the Secular Cathedrals*, CBMLC, 17 (London, 2023).
———, 'John Erghome and the Library of the Austin Friars of York', in C. Saunders and R. Lawrie (eds), *Middle English Manuscripts and Their Legacies: A Volume in Honour of Ian Doyle* (Leiden, 2022), pp. 96–117.
———, 'The Chronicle of Ralph of Coggeshall: Publication and Censorship in Angevin England', in *The Art of Publication from the Ninth to the Sixteenth Centuries*, ed. Samu Niskanen and Valentina Rovere (Turnhout, forthcoming).
———, *The Libraries of the Cathedral Priory of Christ Church, Canterbury*, CBMLC, forthcoming.

Index of Manuscripts

Entries in italics refer to images

General Index

Entries in italics refer to images